DATE DUE			
Feb2 78			

Esquire's
Fashions for Today

Esquire's
Fashions for Today

by Bill Gale and the Editors of *Esquire* Magazine

Illustrated by Gail Hicks

1817

HARPER & ROW, PUBLISHERS

New York, Evanston, San Francisco, London

3 9/.071
21/3 f
8 5-792
Nov. 1973

FIRST EDITION

Designed by Patricia Dunbar

Library of Congress Cataloging in Publication Data
Gale, Bill.
    Fashions for today.
    Half-title: Esquire's fashions for today.
    1. Men's clothing. 2. Fashion. I. Esquire.
II. Title. III. Title: Esquire's fashions for today.
TT617.G35   391'.07'1   70-181617
ISBN 0-06-011184-4

Contents

8

Casual Outerwear 101

An Outerwear Vocabulary—How to Take Care of Casual Outerwear

9

Sportswear 107

For the Spectator—Sweater Guide—How to Take Care of Your Sweaters—Active Sportswear—Skiing—Tennis—Sailing (Boating) —Swimming—Golf—Sports-Car Driving—Horseback Riding— Hunting—Fishing (Trout)—Bicycling—Keeping Fit

10

Weddings and Formal Evening Wear 135

Who Pays for What?—What's Worn When?—The Formal Daytime Wedding (Before 6 P.M.)—The Semiformal Daytime Wedding —The Informal Day or Evening Wedding—The Formal Evening Wedding (After 6 P.M.)—The Semiformal Evening Wedding—The Summer Evening Formal Wedding—The Summer Evening Semiformal Wedding—The Garden Wedding—A Final Checklist for the Groom-to-Be—The Best Man—Chief Usher—Ushers—Bride's Father—Bridegroom's Father—The Wedding—Enter the Bride— The Reception—Dancing—Formal Evening Wear

11

Accessories 153

Jewelry—Glasses—Belts and Suspenders—Handkerchiefs—Neckerchiefs—Scarves—Grooming Aids

12

Travel   169

13

From Jeans to Jobs   185

14

How to Remove Spots and Stains   193

Glossary   201

Index   240

Introduction

Every revolution has its landmarks.
The American, Bunker Hill.
The French, the Bastille.
The Russian, the Winter Palace.
The Peacock, Carnaby Street.
. . . And every revolution has its heroes, who invariably wind up with a chestful of beribboned medals. But Glasgow-born (1938) John Stephen, uncrowned "King of Carnaby Street," has wound up with a blue Rolls-Royce, a burgundy Cadillac, a sable-colored Aston Martin, and business tentacles that reach out to America, Canada, Sweden, Norway, France, Germany and Switzerland.

So it was not surprising when, in 1969, the prestigious *London Times* listing of the one hundred "Makers of the Twentieth Century" put the "King of Carnaby Street" under the S's along with Gertrude Stein, Igor Stravinsky, Erich von Stroheim and President Sukarno. It was only fitting and proper.

For it was the opening of Stephen's first Carnaby Street boutique in 1957 that set off the first tremors of the Peacock Revolution, which soon transformed that once sleepy backwater behind Regent Street into one of the country's Grade A tourist attractions, ranking at the top of the list along with the changing of the Guard at Buckingham Palace and the Beefeaters at the Tower of London. Journalists the world over tagged Carnaby Street "the birthplace of swinging London," and Stephen's pop clothing, picked up and popularized by idolized singing groups, became the nucleus of a new counterculture.

For the first time in history, fashion influence was starting at the bottom of the social ladder and working upward, rather than the reverse. For the first time in this century, men's fashions were generating more excitement and attracting more press coverage than women's. From out of the working class swaggered the new Beau Brummels, the first peacocks of the new pop society.

At a time when Great Britain had skidded into a back seat as a world power, Carnaby Street made her a force to be reckoned with in the weighty world of international fashion. With the world rocking to the beat of the Beatles, Carnaby Street persuaded staid London to toss its bowler hat into the air, its black umbrella into the Thames, and to step out as the swingingest swinger of them all. As Anthony King-Feacon of the *London Times* put it: "Carnaby Street has done us all a vast unreturnable favor—it put us on the map!" Then, warming up to his subject, he continued: "Carnaby Street flinted a spark against the dry and decrepit tinder of the menswear industry and caused such flames as had never been seen before."

By the seventies, however, the smoke had cleared away, and after several seasons of frenetic change, fashions had sensibly settled down. And from out of the frenzy and fury of the fashion revolution evolved today's clothes, full of spirit and imagination— our guarantee that men's fashions will never be dull again.

Certainly, the history of men's fashions has never been dull. There isn't, for example, an article of apparel you wear that doesn't have a story to tell.

The bow on your hatband, for instance, is a carry-over from the battlefield. Cavaliers would wear their ladies' plumes in their headgear, always on the left side (where they still are today) to keep them out of the way of the sword.

And when you take your hat off as a salutatory gesture, you are emulating knights in armor who used to raise their visors to show they were friends, not foes.

The cravat was launched by a regiment of Croats who, fresh from battles with the Turks, went to serve with the French. King Louis XIV noticed their fancy neckgear and took to wearing a cloth around his throat—the word *Croat* being twisted into *cravat*—and the style soon was adopted permanently with the first formation of the dashing regiment of Royal Cravattes.

The raglan sleeve also got its start on the battlefield. When Lord Raglan was leading troops in the Crimean War it was cold, and he devised an outer garment for his men: potato sacks slit at the neck and slashed diagonally at the corners. It made a free-swinging shoulder that proved highly practical.

And so it goes. These little niceties of dress (and not always so nice, either, if you consider that Napoleon invented the buttons on coat sleeves to keep his men from wiping their noses on them) go back to many a tough campaign, and to many a rough customer, rather than to the cutting room or salon.

The four-in-hand tie dates back to the days of the coach-and-four in England. The men on top of the box of the coach were among the first to wear the tie knotted, hence the name four-in-hand.

Lapels on jackets are derived from early military uniforms. Soldiers, wanting to be comfortable, unfastened the upper buttons of the high-collared tunics and rolled back each side. The custom gradually affected civilian fashions and jackets were made with lapels. The notch indicated the break of the collar. Even the buttonhole of the tunic, which was fastened high at the neck, has been retained.

Vents in jackets have a military heritage, too. When a man was on horseback, the slit in the tails of his coat permitted it to fall on each side of the horse. The vent, therefore, continues to appear on all riding jackets for this same reason. It was carried over into sports jackets and business suits, and it makes the trouser pockets more readily accessible. Nowadays you can reach into your pockets without unfastening the buttons of your jacket or putting it out of place. For this convenience you can thank horses.

Cuffs on trousers came into being for practical reasons. Straps attached to the bottoms of trousers of military uniforms used to hold them down. With the disappearance of straps, plain-bottom trousers came into fashion, and when men would walk through the open country they'd habitually turn the bottoms up to avoid brambles and underbrush.

The sweater was originally designed to make the wearer sweat. Or at least that's what it did, and that's how it got its name.

The velvet collar of the chesterfield coat is not the dandified accouterment it may seem. During the French Revolution, those in other countries who wished to express disapproval of the executions added black velvet collars to their coats as a mark of mourning. It has since become a mark of fashion.

The original cutaway coat was the riding coat of the country gentleman, and it was cut away in front to free his knees. During the industrial revolution it was adopted for town wear by newly rich factory owners who wanted to look like landed gentry. The buttons on the back were for looping the tails so they wouldn't get in the way when riding.

The blazer first saw the light of day aboard H.M.S. *Blazer*. After looking over his men, and not being too pleased with the unkempt lot he saw, the captain gave them metal-buttoned blue serge jackets to wear.

There are countless such stories about the details of men's clothing. Like all arts, fashion has a history, and every age contributes its share. What our contribution might be is anybody's guess. Loafers? Jeans? Whatever it is, we'll leave it to future historians. What we're concerned with here is how to make the most of today's clothes. How to look smartly turned out in a natural, offhanded sort of way. Effortlessly right.

That, in brief, is the purpose of this book.

CHAPTER ONE

The Art of Wearing Clothes

THE art of wearing clothes, of presenting an appearance of elegance and taste to the eye of the beholder, of being appropriately clad for the occasion, can be summed up quite simply: *Wear* your clothes, don't let them wear *you!*

But it's advice that's far easier to give than to follow—as a lot of men have found to their sorrow. And the right effect has been more difficult to achieve during the decade of the sixties—late, but not lamented much—than at any time since the last decade of the eighteenth century. Wretched excess marked the fashions for men in both ten-year spans. The dandies of that earlier era were often called *Incroyables,* which is French for "Unbelievables"!

We've seen some fairly unbelievable fashions ourselves in recent years, variously called the Peacock Revolution and the Costume Party. But on sober reflection, I can't honestly say that I either regret or deplore a decade that brought so much excitement and fresh thinking to fashion. It was long overdue, in my estimation, and men needed to be thoroughly shaken out of their stodgy, unimaginative ways of dressing. If, in the course of this revolution, things got a little out of hand here and there, well—revolutions were ever thus!

Highly developed senses of humor and proportion were absolute requirements for living through it all. Unfortunately, not everybody has these faculties, either by birth or by acquisition. But the men who started out well dressed stayed that way. They viewed the farthest-out fashions with amusement, not alarm, and out of the welter of new ideas they were bombarded with chose only those things which suited them and their sense of fitness.

That, my friends, is what is known as true elegance.

THE INDESTRUCTIBILITY OF ELEGANCE

True elegance *is* indestructible. It never dies; it's always there to be seen, not stared at, if you look hard enough. Even when the woods and streets are full of fashions that seem *meant* to be stared at (and lots of them are), you'll still find a certain amount of elegance around.

"Beau" Brummell, a man of impeccable taste, wielded more power over fashion and fashionable men during his day than anyone had since Petronius Arbiter in Nero's Rome. Brummell's famous observation that "When John Bull turns to look after you, you are not well dressed, but either too stiff, too tight or too fashionable" is true today, and it's a safe bet that John Doe feels the same way about it. It's interesting that Brummell's star rose in the firmament of fashion as an almost direct reaction to the too fashionable *Incroyables* and their predecessors the members of London's Macaroni Club. His legacy to us—still valid after more than a century and a half—is that true elegance is simplicity of taste.

Of course, there's more to it than that. An elegant, well-dressed man must have a sense of proportion. Proportion not only from the standpoint of physical measurement (the correct length of a coat that suits *him* primarily and follows any arbitrary dicta of fashion only secondarily, for example) but also proportion in the sense of appropriate dress for the time, the place and the occasion. He's more likely to be underdressed than overdressed, although he manages to hit the ideal squarely in the bull's-eye more often than not.

His sense of proportion extends to the care of both his clothes and himself. He views his wardrobe as the kind of investment that should be protected, but never to the point of fixation. Attention to detail is one thing, fussing over trifles quite another. He views the framework which he covers with his clothes as an integral part of elegance, and keeps himself trim and fit with proper exercise and diet as a natural further protection of his investment. Inspired (and expensive) tailoring can conceal a multitude of sins committed at the table, but in the long run you're better off—both physically *and* financially— keeping yourself in shape.

financial—that finally brought Beau Brummell to his ruin. He owed enormous debts—which he couldn't pay—to, among others, the tailors, hatters, bootmakers and other artisans whose expertise had brought his impeccable taste to perfection. And he got too fat and sloppy to look good in his clothes anyhow.

THE RELAXATION OF RIGID RULES

A very positive plus that appeared out of the maelstrom of sixties fashion was the relaxation of rules that used to be so rigid that you even *bent* them at your peril! You remember, things like: "Colored shirts—pale blues, yellows and, perhaps, pink—may be worn to the office, but a gentleman *always* wears a white shirt in the evening." Or: "Black patent leather pumps are the *only* correct footwear for evening clothes."

Most of these edicts belong right where you can find them today: in old movies on the Late Late Show.

Probably the only occasions for which the rules still apply are ritual in character: formal and semiformal weddings, for instance. (And I doubt that the most liberated man would wear a bright red shirt to a funeral.) Even informal weddings are not what they used to be. The father of the bride at a very posh, but very informal, summer country wedding not long ago turned up in an elegant pair of printed velvet pants. When is the last time *you* remember seeing something like that?

And yet, given the time, the place and the barefoot bride, why not? Or if a man feels like wearing a bright-striped shirt to the office, why on earth shouldn't he? Men in so-called creative fields, like advertising, publishing or the communications media, have long been allowed leeway in their choice of dress. But even more conservative businesses such as banks and insurance companies have shown definite signs of letting down the bars a bit and permitting rather more self-expression in dress.

THE ROOT OF ALL THIS GOOD AND EVIL

Where did all this "peacock urge" for self-expression come from? Like it or not, it all started with "the kids" and percolated upward to their fathers and grandfathers—in, granted, rather modified form. The main impetus of the movement began in England, where young men with new-found financial freedom began to demand sartorial freedom to match, and started to dress to suit themselves. Which was, to their elders' horror, in clothes that fitted the body more closely, that were far more colorful, and that suited the more relaxed life-style that has become everybody's goal. Manufacturers on *both* sides of the Atlantic were slow to pick up the message, giving rise to the proliferation of boutiques where these young men could buy what they wanted—notably in Carnaby Street. (Which remains to this day a bad word among a lot of people who swallowed all the ideas whole and got a bad case of indigestion in both fashion and finance as a result.)

There were, however, those who heard the message loud and clear; they were the men with the kind of creativity that is always looking for a new outlet, and they found it during . . .

THE DECADE OF THE "NAME DESIGNER"

. . . a continuing influence on fashion. Hardy Amies. Bill Blass. Pierre Cardin. Oleg Cassini. Nino Cerruti. Tom Gilbey. Peter Golding. Angelo Litrico. Carlo Palazzi. John Weitz. Uncounted—and uncountable—others. How many of them were household words around *your* home, back around 1960? These were some of the pioneers who broke the first ground in redesigning the man of the sixties, the seventies and the foreseeable future, from top to bottom.

Some, of course, were already familiar to the distaff members of your household. And although none of them has ever designed exclusively for the young men who were demanding the big change in fashion, they've acknowledged almost to a man that their primary inspiration came from the young. In his book, *ABC of Men's Fashion*, Hardy Amies said: "As regards tastes and styles, I am not sure that the younger man today does not know more than his elders." And he has translated the solid tradition of Savile Row tailoring into more readily accessible fashion that is both ageless and classless. Speaking at an *Esquire* Designers' Conference, Bill Blass remarked: "Although, theoretically, the clothes that I make are for what I feel is the decidedly neglected man over thirty, there is no doubt that the young are the inspiration for clothes today." His all-American look emphasizes adaptability, comfort, color and bold masculinity. At that same conference, Pierre Cardin, whose collection ideas range from dressing a present-day dandy to outfitting a space-age astronaut, declared: "I do not pretend to design for everyone, because habits are difficult to change. So I started with young people; in life, you must always start with the young because they can wear anything. That is why I always look to the future, and not behind me."

Well, none of them has *ever* looked back! And they've been joined in their missionary work—which is a dedication to making us all look better than we ever have before—by multitudes of other creative minds, each with his own point of view, each with something to contribute.

TALENT IS NOT A GEOGRAPHIC CONDITION

At the beginning of the sixties, men's fashion could be comfortably contained in a "Golden Triangle"—London, Paris, Rome. In the course of recent years, however, terrific new design talents have surfaced in very nearly every village, town or city you ever heard of, and some you probably haven't. Scandinavia, from Norway to Finland—with intermediate stops in Sweden and Denmark—has produced designers of unexpectedly light and lighthearted sports and beachwear, to say nothing of their native knack with leathers and furs. Paris remains the French fashion magnet for men, whether for *haute couture* houses like Lanvin and Dior (both of whom now produce designs for men as well as women) or for boutique and ready-to-wear items plus all the in-between operations. But the south of France, notably St. Tropez, is a summer bellwether for the fads and fancies of the following winter resort season. Spain has a small but growing fashion industry, particularly in Barcelona, where, as with their northernmost neighbors, leathers and beachwear hold the spotlight.

When it comes to artistic endeavor of any kind, the soil of Italy has always been fertile ground—and fashion is no exception. From Rome to Florence, from Milan to Venice to Parma to Parabiago, new designers with innovative ideas seem to spring up every day, and in every area of fashion from hats to shoes and back! London holds its own as well with fashion, as far-out or as establishment as you could wish, available on demand. And enough new talents have emerged in Greece to warrant the recent formation of the Hellenic Fashion Institute in Athens.

THE WOMAN'S PREROGATIVE

Nor is the business of men's fashion For Men Only anymore. In a movement that actually predated much of the Women's Lib drive, ladies with taste, discrimination and talent have managed to make their voices heard. And again, why not? Not every woman is endowed with these qualities, any more than every man is, but I'll bet if you think about it, you know more men who take their wives' advice in such matters than men who don't!

Take, for instance, Karen Hellemaa, the resident genius at Fri-itala-Finland, who comes up with great-looking ideas in leather and fur season after season. Or Copenhagen's Margit Brandt, who uses unusual fabrics for her relaxed-looking tailored clothes and sportswear. In Athens, Elly Abravanel takes imaginative advantage of native Greek designs and local fabrications in her beachwear collections. Moya Bowler never seems to be at a loss for a new look in the shoes she designs for Sids in London. Mila Schön, a well-known name in distaff designs, uses many of the same individual fabrics in her women's collection and in her newly established men's line. At her studio in Venice, Roberta di Camerino produces her own print designs for scarves, and designs extraordinarily masculine leather accessories.

HOW COME ALL THIS CREATIVITY, ALL OF A SUDDEN?

I don't think it was quite as sudden as it may have seemed to those of you who were still encased in your gray flannel natural shoulder suits! Those of us who are in the fashion field are, naturally, aware of trends before they become visible to the naked eye—which is one reason why we're in the fashion business to begin with. But all the new ideas which have resulted from all the new talents were, I think, a definite reflection of the fact that there was widespread —if unrecognized—dissatisfaction with the status quo in men's clothing. A lot of men didn't appear to realize it until they were faced with these new ideas, these new approaches to dress, and the multiplicity of options that were suddenly open to them.

And that, of course, is the biggest of all the plusses that have emerged from this Peacock Revolution: the enormous *variety of choice* that today's man has when it comes to clothes.

Much of the correspondence we receive in *Esquire*'s fashion department still seeks cut-and dried answers to questions like "What is the maximum width of a tie?" or "How deep should the cuff on your trousers be?" And the answer, these days, is that there just *isn't* any one answer! The day when some self-proclaimed pundit handed down incontrovertible edicts from fashion's own Mount Olympus is long gone. Now it's a matter of personal taste and common sense—which probably comes harder to a lot of men than a flat-out rule would. My own rule for dilemmas is: When in doubt, ask. Ask your wife; ask your favorite salesman at the shop or store where you buy your clothes; ask your friends. Under *no* circumstances should you accept advice from anyone who's trying to make points with you, or—it shouldn't be necessary to say—from your worst enemy! Take a good, solid look at yourself in the fitting room mirror, as objective a look as you can manage (and few of us are completely objective about our reflected image). If you hear or read somewhere that a five-inch tie with a Windsor knot is the *only* smart thing to wear this season, but the tie's knot is bigger than your whole head, just face the fact that you'll have to sacrifice a little "smartness" in order to look *your* best. That's what fashion's all about today. And what it *should* have been about all along.

THE LEISURED LIFE-STYLE:
ANOTHER ASPECT OF FASHION

As this is written, there is a great deal of talk about shortened or staggered work hours and days, and the four-day work week. Much of the talk is already being matched by corporate action.

Which all adds up to considerably more leisure and play time for all of us—and, increasingly, we're dressing for it. The stereotyped Britisher who "dressed for dinner" deep in the jungle, complete with black tie and starched gates-ajar collar, is being replaced by men like you and me who come home from our work and "dress for dinner" in comfortable, colorful clothes that are made for the purpose: to be relaxed in. The same attitude holds true for whatever leisure time you may have either at the traditional weekend or midweek, whenever your schedule permits.

I am happy to report, what's more, that there are strong indications that more of you are *doing* something with that added leisure time. (Always excepting the avid pro-sport fan who refuses to flex a muscle that might remove him from his television set during the season—yet another stereotype.) But active sportsmen are becoming more prevalent. There are more tennis players on more tennis courts—even indoor courts for year-round play; there are more golfers than ever all across the country; there's an explosion in the boating fraternity, both in blue-water sailors and in power-boat skippers; ardent skiers are flying to South America when the snows melt in this hemisphere, or taking to water-skiing to tide them over. Hiking, climbing, camping and bicycling are the rediscovered dynamics of activists in the ecology movement.

What's all this got to do with fashion? Two things. One is that you *must* be comfortably and appropriately dressed for whatever activity you want to engage in, to engage in it well. The pro golfers have led the way to brilliant, offbeat color as well as comfort on the course. The USLTA softened their rules a couple of years ago to permit light blue and yellow on even the most exclusive courts, but most tennis players, pro or amateur, stick to regulation whites. Again, though, it's got to be *comfortable!* Practicality and comfort are the basic ideas behind almost any kind of sportswear—but more and more men are realizing that their sports clothes don't have to be drab or ugly to be practical and comfortable. And so do the men who make the stuff.

The second advantage that sports have from the fashion standpoint is that almost any physical activity is, like it or not, *exercise*: coupled with a proper diet, it's bound to make you look better and feel better than a sedentary, pencil-pushing, TV-watching existence can. In my own opinion, there is *nothing* quite as boring as "hup-two"-type calisthenics, but an ever-growing number of urban males are enrolling in exercise classes, either to help keep themselves in shape in between their bouts with their own particular sport, or for simple vanity's sake. A lean, muscular frame wears its clothes better than a fat, pudgy one—and that's the truth.

THE GROOMING GAME: A WHOLE NEW WORLD

It's difficult to pinpoint just when the bars broke down and allowed men to look their best even with artificial aids. During the fifties just about all the American male could qualify for was what my grandmother called "not handsome, but sweet and clean." Soap, water, a short haircut and a close shave was about all the law allowed. Provided some foolhardy friend had given him some aftershave, a miserly dab of it might be used by a more daring type.

I heard a bit of doggerel once about a man not minding what he looked like since he didn't have to see himself. What a burden to place on your friends and fellowmen! A man owes it to others, as well as himself, to look the best he can. And for the first time in centuries he's got a plethora of products to help him do it, and he's becoming less and less shy about using them.

Hair Today—Gone Tomorrow?

Probably the most controversial subject in grooming during the sixties was hair. When the young began to grow their own, the collective scream from their elders was deafening. As the decade wore on, though, even older men began to see that something between the crew cut and the excessive lengths sported by some were infinitely more flattering. They usually started with sideburns, then abandoned the bowl-cut look in back; and many graduated to mustaches and beards. Unlike their children (who honesty compels me to admit often went too far), most mature men had the wit and common sense to place themselves in the hands of pros to have their hair properly trimmed. Enter the men's hair stylist, who is trained to help you make the most of what you grow. Enter, as well, quantities of fake hair: long wigs to disguise GI haircuts on weekends; sideburns to wear while your own grew in; beards and mustaches, either to decide what style suited you best or to wear on your own time if your employer disallowed facial decorations at work. It was fun while it lasted, but there are definite signs of a new trend a-coming, for shorter hair once more. It may be a while before we see a crew cut again. But maybe the next real startler will be a Yul Brynner-style shaved pate.

The Skin Game

Nobody but a damn fool would spend eight hours in the sun on his first day at the beach—which doesn't preclude the presence of a lot of damn fools in the world. But that, in effect, is what a lot of us used to do: run from steam-heated offices into windy, wintry cold, from air-conditioned places into noonday sun, without anything to protect our skins. Many of our wives knew we were sneaking smitches of their creams or lotions when our faces began to feel like incipient smithereens, but it was a pretty well-kept secret. Then the proverbial light bulb went on over the heads of skin specialists and cosmetic manufacturers, and the men's toiletries industry was born. After a bit of initial resistance it began to boom, for a simple reason: these new products make you feel good and look good—and not necessarily in that order. Now there are whole lines of products, all in the same masculine scent that you've tried and liked, and each with a specific chore to perform, designed to help you make the most of what you've got. Did you think it was all that orange juice that suddenly produced a whole new breed of better-looking men? No, we've just realized that a man's success can depend on the impression he creates, just as a woman's does. To put it in crasser, more commercial terms, you have a product—yourself—to put over. If you look full of well-being, vigor and confidence, you're going to feel that way. And if you feel awful, you don't *have* to look it!

THE SCIENTIFIC PRESENCE ON THE
FASHION SCENE

Fashion is an art, right? Right. Wearing clothes well is an art, too
—right? Right. But you couldn't do it nearly as well without the
contributions science has made to men's fashions: greater practicality, greater variety of choice, and greater availability of good
fashion to every man.

Technology has become a dirty word in recent years to those
who evidently equate it solely with military hardware, industrial
complexes, the computer culture, and the like. But it's technology
that has made it possible to spend less time and money on clothes,
and without sacrificing an iota of fashion. Manmade fibers, plus a
myriad of technological processes and developments, have resulted
in things like wash-and-wear shirts and durable-press pants which
are eliminating big laundry bills (except, perhaps, for the coins in
the automatic washer and dryer). Tailored clothing keeps its
shape and its fresh-from-the-shop look longer. Ties treated with
spot repellent will shed any soup you may spill. Boots and shoes
are easier to keep clean and looking polished. "Antistatic" socks
which prevent trouser cling are available. Fabric can be made to
stretch, breathe, keep a crease—almost anything it has to do to
make a garment workable and wearable. And the list is endless!

As for knits, they're a whole new category of minor miracles
all by themselves! Knit shirts, trousers, sports jackets, suits, outercoats—they belong to one of the biggest breakthroughs in comfort,
easy care and good looks to come along in years. Knits are a classic
example of creative talent coupled with technology which make
the art of wearing clothes easier than it's ever been before.

THE SUMMING UP

All right, then, to what end have all these revolutionary new ideas
brought us?

Anyone with half an eye knows that we are *not* living in the
best of all possible worlds, as that fathead Candide declared sun-

nily in the face of fire, flood, earthquake, and sundry other disasters. But in the rather narrower context of fashion, it's the best world that's been possible *up to now*. And beyond the wildest surmises of our forebears. No one knows what tomorrow, or next year, or even the twenty-first century may bring—so let's enjoy our freedom in fashion while we may.

And what's to enjoy is this: No one can tell you anymore what you *must* wear to be correct, well-dressed, fashionable or whatever you aspire to be. There are far too many alternatives open to all of us for that. The kings and princes of history may have had clothing "for all seasons," but we're the first to neither bow to the seasons to be comfortable, nor spend a king's ransom to do it. We may have rediscovered the olfactory pleasures of masculine scent, but we weren't forced to because we stank in the first place.

In short, we have it in us—and available to us—to be the best-looking, best-dressed, most colorful and most comfortable generation of men the world has ever known.

Let's make the most of it.

CHAPTER TWO

Suits

BEFORE we get into the area of what style of suit is most flattering to your physique, let's consider what any really good suit of clothes should offer a man be he ectomorph, endomorph, or mesomorph. In short, let's deal with the verities that comprise the yardstick by which you should judge any suit you're planning to buy.

WHAT TO LOOK FOR WHEN BUYING A SUIT

Certainly, fit is the most important element in creating a well-dressed man; you just don't stand a chance of looking carefully turned out if your clothes don't fit, no matter what silhouette you choose or how much money you spend. What you aim for is a look of ease and naturalness, and furthermore your suit must remain comfortable and good-looking when you're in motion, not just when you're standing still in front of the fitter's mirror. So don't just stand there like a ramrod. Slip your wallet into your inside jacket pocket (if that's where you customarily carry it, it certainly should be there when you're trying on a new suit) . . . button the jacket . . . walk about and sit down. Remember, comfort is as essential to fashion as vermouth is to a martini.

Now, on to the verities:

Collar

It should fit low and close around the neck, showing at least half an inch of shirt collar in the back. And no matter how much or how wide you wave your arms, it shouldn't gape or fall away from your neck. If the suit collar doesn't hug your neck smoothly, it's going to make the whole jacket appear lopsided.

16

RISE OF COLLAR

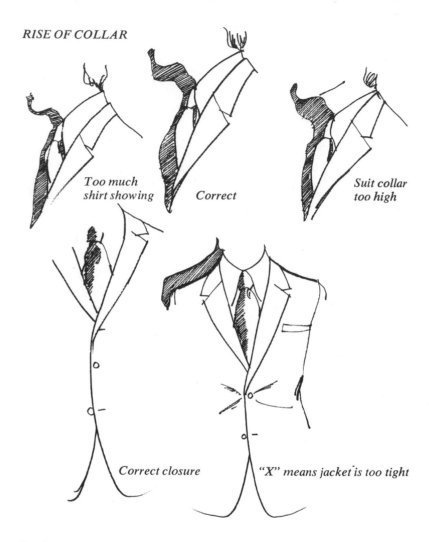

Too much
shirt showing

Correct

Suit collar
too high

Correct closure

"X" means jacket is too tight

Pockets

Flat and smooth—there's no other way for a pocket to be. If it hangs away from your jacket or ripples with wrinkles, it probably doesn't have any interlining. Ergo, an inferior suit of clothes.

Shoulders

Watch for a horizontal ripple below the base of the neck. It's a sure sign that material should be cut away across the top of the shoulder. And if when you're standing straight there are tension lines pulling across the shoulder blades, the back is too tight and must be let out a little.

Waist

This is the acid test: button the jacket and look for X-shaped lines radiating out from the top button(s). If they're too pronounced, the waist should be let out. Another sign that the waist is too tight: horizontal creases will appear in the small of the back.

Waistband

This is a toughie since the unsightly roll-over doesn't show up until you've worn the suit two or three times. So we suggest you ask your salesman if the waistband has an inner or double curtain lining, which is the only built-in insurance against the waistband roll-over that can make even a washboard-flat stomach look suspiciously paunchy.

Lapels

No subtlety here—just grab hold and *squeeze*. The lapel should snap back with nary a wrinkle provided the suit has good interlining.

Sleeves

Properly cut sleeves are full at the top, or sleevehead, and taper to the cuff. How much tapering they do usually depends on two things: the dictates of fashion and your physique. When it seems the two are in open conflict, strike up a compromise, giving, of course, the special requirements of your physique top priority. (More about that a few pages on.) For now, simply remember that the top of a sleeve must never seem "pruned" with wrinkles

LAPELS

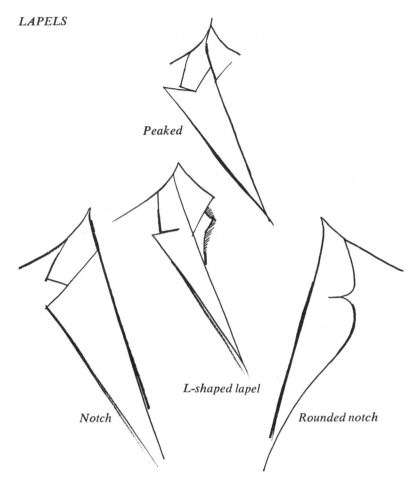

Peaked

L-shaped lapel

Notch

Rounded notch

but should give your arm a smooth, rounded appearance. And of course your sleeves should always be pressed sans crease.

So far as sleeve length goes, tradition still counts for something, which is another way of saying that the jacket sleeve should be cut so that at least half an inch of shirt cuff shows at the wrist when your arm hangs loose (more when your arm is bent). Sleeves should never conceal all linen, no matter what you do with your arms. Nor should they ride up above the top edge of your shirt cuff.

Too much or too little shirt cuff showing is equally undesirable; the former suggesting a hand-me-down and the other giving you a Li'l Abner look.

Armholes

No matter how shaped you want your suit jacket, you also want comfort. So steer clear of the too low armscye (the technical name for lower part of the armhole) that causes the sleeve to bind your arm when you raise it. Years ago women had their iron corsets, a masochistic concession to shapelier garb; some of today's peacocks have submitted to straight-cut suit jackets, assuming discomfort to be essential to a well-shaped suit. Not so. Armholes should ideally be cut high rather than low.

Trousers

The flared trouser is no longer the oddity it was just a few years ago, but the amount of flare, like everything else in today's fashion world, is subject to change. (Currently favored is a width of 19 inches at the knee and 18 to 19 inches at the bottom.) Suffice it to say, how much flare depends in great part on your height and physical proportions.

Whether plain or cuffed, bottoms should hang without a break in front. And the front should be even with the top of the back of the shoe.

So long as a suit is still the suit as we've known it for these many generations, the guidelines above will serve you well. Meantime, however, there is new sartorial territory opened up by the Peacock Revolution and it's high time we explored it.

KNITS AND THEIR HANGTAG JARGON

Knits were little more than a designer's dream as late as the late 1960s, but by the early seventies they were helping to reshape men's apparel. As one fashion reporter put it: "For walking, running, standing, slouching or crouching or cringing, knit is the fabric." In other words, knits are made to move—and travel. A knit suit, for instance, can be practically as unrestricting as a pair of blue jeans. And furthermore, it can be rolled up in a suitcase and worn when unpacked without being pressed. Any slight folds that may develop hang out in minutes.

Knits can now be found in just about every fashion item you want to buy: from suits and sports coats to sport shirts and softly tailored dress shirts, to ties, topcoats, raincoats and even hatbands. And since their development required a whole new technology, knits also spawned a whole new fashion vocabulary for the shopper. It's important you learn some of the hangtag jargon:

Blisters. Raised or dimensional textures of patterns in a double-knit fabric. Highly raised patterns are usually avoided in menswear to escape snagging.

Comfort stretch. The two-way "give" and recovery action in a knitted fabric.

Denier. The unit of weight indicating the size of a fiber filament. The higher the number, the heavier the yarn.

Double knits. Clothing made of jersey yarn knitted on a circular machine with a double set of needles. Double knits can be solid, patterned or textured, and in texture can go from very thin to broad corduroy-like effects. The cloth is firm and heavy.

Gauge. Represents the number of needles per inch of width. The greater the number, the closer and finer the knit.

Jacquard. A system of knitting complicated patterns. Typical jacquards: paisley, tartan plaids, geometrics, etc.

Pilling. The formation of little fuzz balls on the surface of a fabric caused by the rubbing off of loose ends of the fiber.

Raschel. The fabrics can be similar to warp-knit tricots, but the machine itself has greater knitting versatility in terms of the weights, textures and stitch variety it can produce. Two-way comfort stretch can be engineered into the fabric. Weights range from shirtings to coatings.

Snagging. The pulling out of a single end of yarn in a knitted fabric. It can usually be punched back into place. Deeply textured fabrics can be subject to snagging.

Sweater knits. As the name suggests, they're knit the way sweaters are and have a tendency to bag unless bonded. Used for the most part in outfits for leisure wear.

Tricot. A warp-knit fabric with each side different. Tricot knits are very tough and highly resistant to damage from tearing or snagging. Two-way stretch can be engineered into the fabric. Weights range from shirtings to jeans.

Warp knits. Made on flatbed machines via a series of yarns looped together to form lengthwise rows of fabrics. Warp knits are noted for their high resistance to running when snagged and to unraveling when cut or ripped. The main menswear warp knits are tricots and raschels.

Quite frankly, most but not all of the kinks are out of knits at this writing. Still, their plusses appear to outweigh the few minuses in the opinion of the most fashion-conscious men. (And with the technological know-how of the seventies, by the time you've got your hands on this book, the last few kinks will very likely have been "unkinked.")

THE CARE OF KNITS

As for the care and feeding of your knits, check the hangtag for specific instructions. Meanwhile here are a few pointers (a couple of which you won't find on any hangtag):

Knits cannot be rewoven. So to correct a snag, *don't* clip it off. Instead thread a needle with snagged material and pull it through the snag to the other side.

Double knits can be altered just as woven fabrics can. But, as you would with woven fabrics, you should check the label to see if the garment is permanent press. If so, it can be shortened but not lengthened.

Dry clean your knit suit or sports jacket. *Never*, under any circumstances, use a hot iron on a knit fabric.

Cuffs aren't advisable on knit pants. Since the fabric is too soft to support itself, cuffs tend to flop over.

THE BLAZER SUIT

Do you really know what it is? Lots of men don't, for the simple reason that the blazer sports jacket whence this suit concept came is no longer the strictly navy blue brass-buttoned affair it once was. Today a blazer can come in any color or any pattern; its buttons may be metallic, bone or a plastic of a contrasting color. So exactly what is a blazer suit? Answer: a suit whose jacket is sporty enough to do yeoman duty as a blazer sports jacket, specifically by virtue of its cut, fabric and trim (preferably all three, but two out of three will suffice). And getting right down to the nitty-gritty, that means:

Cut

The blazer suit jacket has a little more flair than the usual suit jacket. This extra flair may come via something like a neat cuff on the sleeve, or scalloped-flap pockets. Whatever it may be, it's the extra flair that makes this particular suit jacket sporty enough to wear as a sports jacket . . . and yet it is never extreme, it never looks too sporty with trousers.

Fabric

The blazer suit must be in one of the many fabrics from which a blazer sports jacket may be made. And the list, of course, is all but inexhaustible: flannel, linen, corduroy, cotton, wool twill, hopsack, velvet, denim, double knit, et cetera.

Trim

More often than not, the distinguishing trim is to be found in the jacket's buttons. Still, it may be in the guise of, say, a suede trim around the buttonholes or pockets, or decorative stitching of a contrasting color.

Get the picture? What the blazer suit spells is a jacket that offers the sports jacket some stiff competition—and you a suit that is extremely smart-looking and practical. It is, in short, a slightly sportier-looking suit and today it would be possible for 75 percent of the suits in a man's wardrobe to be blazer suits.

THE CASUAL SUIT

Or the Easy Suit. Or the Leisure Suit. Or the Unconstructed (no lining) Suit. It has a host of aliases and comes in a variety of styles —shirt suit, tunic suit, vest suit, sweater suit, jean suit, jump suit, safari suit, et cetera—each one allowing the wearer plenty of comfort and a tantalizing opportunity for self-expression. As the name suggests, its purpose in life is to make the wearer look and feel great when he's not doing anything in particular. It's not every man's idea of a suit but a suit it is, and the styles that more closely approximate a conventional suit are sometimes accepted for business wear in those areas (the creative department of an advertising agency, for instance) that often serve as incubators for avant-garde fashion.

Very often they're easy-going knits that fit like a second skin, but they also come in every possible fabric from sturdy canvas, denim and wool tweed, to linen, suede and soft chamois. And most often they show a marked descent from the military uniform (everything from World War I to the French Foreign Legion) and the working garb of the cowboy.

Are they for you? Only you can answer that one. To be more specific, you *and* a full-length mirror. For these free-and-easy styles are meant for a lithe, youthful body. Note we refer to the youth of the body rather than the man's calendar years. A twenty-two-year-old with a thickening waistline will look plenty sad in an easy suit with an all-around belt pointing up his premature portliness, while a trim, flat-bellied forty-year-old can wear the same outfit with panache to spare. So if the urge to don a casual suit is strong enough but you're not trim enough, pare away the excess inches and go to it.

Even taking into account their avant-garde styling (which in some instances has earned them the tag *nonsuit*), the basic rules that apply to choosing a suit for your physical type apply to the casual suit, too. Are here are those rules:

FASHION RULES

The Short Man

What you're striving for—always in all ways—is the illusion of more height. Anything that elongates is good for the short as well as for the fat man. The all-black suit is the tallest of all: use it as an ideal and you may be able to choose casual clothes that seem to be all one color even when they're not. In patterns, vertical designs are of course preferable, and you should use a longer lapel on your jacket. In fact, you'd do well to make the roll go all the way to the button. And yes, avoid the horizontal effect of pocket flaps.

As for trousers, no matter how much flare becomes the vogue, you should steer toward a slimmer, more tapered line. And leave off the cuffs, which tend to create a horizontal line. The combination of minimum flare and no cuff will also give the illusion of a longer foot. Eschew the hip-hugger-style trousers, for they shorten the leg, and it follows that the more leg you show, the longer and leggier you'll appear.

Your suit jacket must never be too long and of course the casual suit—in particular the vest and jump suit—is extremely flattering to you provided you're not carrying around excess poundage.

The Tall, Thin Man

What you're working for is the illusion of more breadth and here contemporary fashions are in your corner, what with all the spirited, look-alive patterns and plaids and overplaids to choose from.

The shoulder of your jacket should be as squared as fashion permits, and no matter what anybody tells you, don't make the mistake of having your suit extremely shaped. Now and then a well-meaning salesman with a bulging midriff will look enviously at your spare frame and decide you should flaunt it. *Don't.* Your jacket should fit rather loosely and be of medium length with wider and lower-cut lapels. (Show as much shirt front as possible.) Trousers should have flare and cuffs to break up the long-legged appearance. The low-rise, hip-hugger style is made to order for you.

Avoid fabrics that cling; opt instead for tweeds and bulk fabrics. If you want a pattern, overplaids, checks and glenurquhart plaids are best.

Accentuate the horizontal with a double-breasted jacket and flapped pockets.

So far as the casual suit is concerned, play it conservative. Avoid the skinny styles and choose, say, a hearty-looking safari suit in suede or linen (fabrics that don't cling). With its wide pockets, wide belt, bold collar, shoulder epaulets (optional), and longish jacket, the safari suit is ideal for your physique. If your arms aren't as beefy as you'd like them to be, start lifting weights or swimming four laps a day—or settle for a safari suit with a long-sleeved jacket. In short, when it comes to the casual suit, think in terms of the loose-fitting top that's worn outside the trousers with a *wide* belt—a combination that cuts off inches by subtracting them from the legs and adding them widthwise.

The Fat Man

All your life you've probably been told to wear a single-breasted suit. It's not necessarily so. On some overweight men the double-breasted style looks most flattering since it may tend to flatten out the abdomen. (Note we say *may*, for a lot depends on how you're proportioned. The point we're trying to make is that there is no set rule here.) On other fat men the single-breasted is best, though the vertical line of the buttons can emphasize the abdomen. So the best thing is to put yourself and your new suit to the test via that brutally frank three-way mirror.

In any event, single- or double-breasted, the shoulders of your suit jacket should be padded slightly to avoid any suggestion of tightness. Don't kid yourself that nipping in the waistline of your jacket will somehow create the illusion of a trimmer midsection; it doesn't work that way. Your jacket should be only slightly shaped and both sleeves and trouser legs should be tapered as much as contemporary fashion permits. (It should go without saying, but we'll say it: avoid the low-rise trouser.) Shun pocket flaps and cuffed trousers, both of which create horizontal effects. The cut of your jacket should be such that the meeting of the collar and the lapel (the gorge) is high up. This will diminish the squatty look that you'll get if they're low-slung.

Gabardines, sharkskins, worsteds—all the smooth suiting fabrics are best for you, in medium and dark colors. Bulky tweeds are off limits, and in summer so are the crinkly seersuckers that give the overweight man a slept-in look. And while you may be tempted to indulge in some of the extroverted patterns, fight it. When it comes to patterns, make yours small and quiet.

Unless you're one of the very unique overweight men who doesn't have a bulging abdomen, save the casual suit for a later date. Or better yet, start dieting, stick to it, and invest in a casual suit—in a smaller size as an incentive to reach your goal.

FABRICS

A surprising number of men who are crammed with knowledge regarding cut and styling features are surprisingly naïve when it comes to fabric facts. All of which indicates a serious lack in their consumer education, inasmuch as each suiting fabric has its own special properties, texture and idiosyncrasies. One that might be a stunner in fall and winter can prove to be a stifler come springtime. Another has an especially posh look but wrinkles easily, adding immeasurably to your pressing bill. So a little fabric knowledge goes a long way toward making you a smart shopper who knows what he wants and why he wants it, whether it be in a ready-made or tailor-made suit.

The following chart capsules the pithy facts for you and you'd do well to commit them to memory or, failing that, take this book shopping with you next time you're out scouting for a new suit.

HOW TO ORDER A TAILOR-MADE SUIT

You pay more and you get more. But every now and then a man falls into the hands of a tailor more intent on projecting *his* image than his customer's personality. This won't happen if you know what you want. All the more reason then that you familiarize yourself with the fabric chart, as well as those basic truths concerning proper fit already covered in this chapter.

Now, assuming you're about to order a tailor-made suit, here are some facts you should be acquainted with inasmuch as your new suit starts out in life as a bolt of cloth awaiting the dictates of you and your friendly tailor.

Lapels

You'll have a choice of lapel styles, so you should learn what they are.

The *notched* lapel is comprised of a broad sideways V-shaped opening midway in the lapel. A staple, this style of lapel just naturally goes along with a natural shoulder suit. A *rounded-notch* lapel is fresher and more sophisticated and more indicative of a tailor-made suit. The *peaked* lapel has a point at its outer edge, thus leaving a gap between the lapel and the bottom of the collar. It's very dressy and its up-and-down lines tend to accent height. The *L-shaped* lapel has no jutting corners, running in a smooth narrow band from lapel around the back of the neck. It, too, emphasizes a slim line.

Pockets

The precise number and style of pockets is a matter between you and your tailor. It's a very satisfactory feeling, we think, to be able to approve or veto a pocket, since on the ready-made suit you have to settle for the ones that come with it. Now, let's focus on the most commonly used styles:

The *flap* pocket, used on suits, jackets or outer coats, is made with a welt seam at the top of the flap. The pocket itself is inside

FABRIC CHART: FALL AND WINTER

TYPE	CONTENT	APPEARANCE	CLEANING	SHAPE DURABILITY	WRINKLES
BEDFORD CORD	All worsted	Ridged, corded	Dry clean	Holds press very well	Resists; minimal; good recovery
CASHMERE AND WOOL	Cashmere and wool	Soft, slightly fuzzy	Dry clean	Holds press briefly	Moderately
CAVALRY TWILL	All worsted	Defined slanted twill	Dry clean	Holds press very well	Resists; minimal; good recovery
CHEVIOT	All worsted	Moderately coarse weave	Dry clean	Holds press fairly well	Readily
CORDUROY	All cotton Cotton and synthetic fiber	Textured, soft	Wash and dry or Dry clean	Holds press fairly well	Resists; minimal; good recovery
FLANNEL	All worsted	Slightly napped surface	Dry clean	Holds press fairly well	Moderately
GABARDINE	All worsted	Fine, twill weave	Dry clean	Holds press very well	Slightly
HOPSACK	All worsted	Coarse, basket-weave effect	Dry clean	Holds press fairly well	Moderately
KNIT	100% polyester All worsted All cotton	Smooth, soft	Dry clean	Holds press remarkably well	Crease-resistant
POLYESTER AND WORSTED	Polyester and worsted	Smooth finish	Dry clean	Holds press very well	Moderately
POLYESTER, WORSTED AND MOHAIR	Polyester, worsted and mohair	Smooth, lustrous	Dry clean	Holds press well	Slightly
SERGE	All worsted	Smooth finish	Dry clean	Holds press very well	Resists; minimal; good recovery

FABRIC CHART: FALL AND WINTER (cont'd)

TYPE	CONTENT	APPEARANCE	CLEANING	SHAPE DURABILITY	WRINKLES
SHARKSKIN	All worsted	Smooth surface, Smooth, slightly 2 colors interwoven	Dry clean	Holds press well	Slightly
SILK AND WORSTED	Silk and worsted	Smooth, shiny	Dry clean	Holds press fairly well	Moderately
TWEED	All wool	Coarse weave, fuzzy surface	Dry clean	Holds press briefly	Readily
VELVET	Cotton, Linen, Nylon, Rayon, Silk	Soft, lustrous	Dry clean	Holds press fairly well	Resists; minimal; good recovery
VELVETEEN	Cotton	Soft, lustrous	Dry clean	Holds press fairly well	Resists; minimal; good recovery
WHIPCORD	All worsted	Visible twill weave	Dry clean	Holds press very well	Slightly
WOOL AND ACRYLIC BLEND	Wool and acrylic fibers	Basket-weave, textured look	Dry clean	Holds press fairly well	Readily
WORSTED (CLEAR-FACED)	All worsted	Closely woven, smooth surface	Dry clean	Holds press very well	Resists; minimal; good recovery
WORSTED (UNFINISHED)	All worsted	Closely woven, slightly napped surface	Dry clean	Holds press well	Resists; minimal; good recovery
WORSTED (STRETCH)	All worsted or worsted plus core-spun (Lycra spandex)	Smooth, closely woven	Dry clean	Has elastic and restorative qualities; holds shape well	Minimal; good recovery

FABRIC CHART: SPRING AND SUMMER

TYPE	CONTENT	APPEARANCE	CLEANING	SHAPE DURABILITY	WRINKLES
CORD	Polyester and cotton	Raised weave, corded	Wash and dry	Holds press fairly well	Moderately
CORDUROY	All cotton Cotton and synthetic fiber	Textured, soft	Wash and dry or Dry clean	Holds press fairly well	Resists; minimal; good recovery
COVERT CLOTH LOOK	Polyester and cotton	Smooth, twill weave	Wash and dry	Holds press fairly well	Moderately
GABARDINE	All wool	Smooth, twill weave	Dry clean	Holds press well	Slightly
HOPSACK	Polyester and cotton	Coarse weave—derived from burlap look, but refined	Dry clean	Holds press fairly well	Readily
KNIT	100% polyester All worsted All cotton	Smooth, soft	Dry clean	Holds press remarkably well	Crease-resistant
LINEN	Linen	Coarse weave	Wash and dry or Dry clean	Holds press briefly	Readily
LINEN LOOK	Polyester and flax	Irregular surface	Wash and dry	Holds press well	Moderately
NUBBY ACETATE	Acetate rayon	Nubby surface, lustrous	Dry clean	Holds press well	Moderately

FABRIC CHART: SPRING AND SUMMER (*cont'd*)

TYPE	CONTENT	APPEARANCE	CLEANING	SHAPE DURABILITY	WRINKLES
OXFORD CLOTH	Polyester and cotton	Basket-weave effect	Wash and dry	Holds press fairly well	Readily
POLYESTER AND ACRYLIC FIBERS	Tropical blend	Smooth, plain close weave	Wash and dry	Holds press well	Moderately
POLYESTER, MOHAIR AND WORSTED	Blend of polyester, mohair and worsted	Smooth, sleek, lustrous	Dry clean	Holds press very well	Moderately
POLYESTER AND RAYON	Tropical blend	Smooth surface, lightweight look	Wash and dry	Holds press well	Moderately
POLYESTER AND WOOL	Tropical blend	Smooth finish	Dry clean	Holds press well	Resists; minimal; good recovery
POLYESTER AND WORSTED	Polyester worsted	Slub and nubbed, some luster, iridescent	Dry clean	Holds press fairly well	Resists; minimal; good recovery
POPLIN	Polyester and cotton	Smooth, close weave	Wash and dry	Holds press fairly well	Moderately
POPLIN	Polyester and rayon	Smooth, close weave	Wash and dry	Holds press fairly well	Moderately
SEERSUCKER	All cotton	Crinkled, porous	Wash and dry	Holds press fairly well	Moderately
SEERSUCKER	Polyester and cotton	Crinkled, porous	Wash and dry	Holds press well	Moderately

FABRIC CHART: SPRING AND SUMMER (*cont'd*)

TYPE	CONTENT	APPEARANCE	CLEANING	SHAPE DURABILITY	WRINKLES
SILK	All silk	Nubby and lustrous, iridescent	Dry clean	Holds press fairly well	Moderately
STRETCH POPLIN	Polyester and cotton plus core-spun (Lycra spandex)	Smooth surface	Dry clean	Holds press fairly well	Resists and good recovery
TRIACETATE AND RAYON	Blend of triacetate and rayon	Smooth, porous	Wash and dry	Holds press fairly well	Readily
VELVET	Cotton Linen Nylon Rayon Silk	Soft, lustrous	Dry clean	Holds press fairly well	Resists; minimal; good recovery
VELVETEEN	Cotton	Soft, lustrous	Dry clean	Holds press fairly well	Resists; minimal; good recovery
WORSTED	Tropical, all worsted	Smooth, porous	Dry clean	Holds press very well	Resists; minimal; good recovery
WORSTED AND MOHAIR	Blend of worsted and mohair	Smooth, lustrous, porous	Dry clean	Holds press very well	Resists; minimal; good recovery

POCKETS

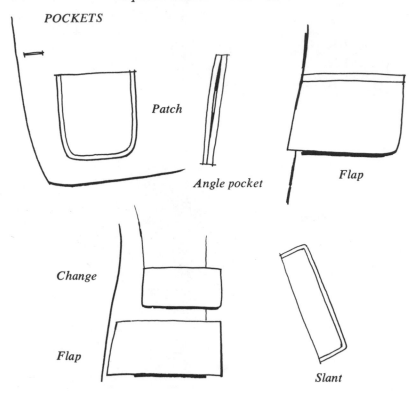

Patch

Angle pocket

Flap

Change

Flap

Slant

the jacket and is made of some other material. Flap pockets are by far the most common type, and sometimes the flap can be tucked neatly inside the pocket, leaving only a slit showing. This is not merely a whimsical practice; it has tangible effects in that it makes the jacket look slimmer. When the flap is tucked in like this, it makes the pocket look very much like another type: the besom pocket.

The *besom* is also an "inside construction," and it is made with a narrow welt seam across the upper and lower edges of the opening. There is no flap to tuck in or leave out, to get creased or wrinkled, halfway stuck in, halfway hanging out. The appearance is always neat and trim.

A *change* pocket, also called a ticket pocket, is a turn-of-the-century innovation that has been revived. It is a small pocket placed above the conventional flap pocket on the right-hand side. English sports coats have them quite often, but they can add an elegant touch to a business suit as well.

A *chest* pocket is no longer considered indispensable and unless you speak up, your tailor just might decide to forget all about it or give you one but with a flap treatment. Ah, but *you* shouldn't forget about it, not if you still have a fondness for a colorful pocket handkerchief. Also keep in mind that if you hanker after a pocket handkerchief, your choice of lapel style had better not be so wide that it all but overlaps the chest pocket.

Another variation is the *hacking* pocket, otherwise known as the slanting or angled pocket. Originally used for riding apparel, it is now a standard feature in suits and sports jackets. The shaped suit is more apt to have it than the straight-line natural shoulder model, because the slanted line tends to accentuate the shaped contours of the former.

The *welt* pocket is the traditional style for the chest pocket in suits and sports jackets. It is placed on the left side next to the lapel and usually sports a chest pocket handkerchief. A narrow strip of fabric is sewn across the top, and whether it is of interior or exterior construction is determined by the style used on the other pockets. An example of a pocket with exterior construction is the widely used patch pocket.

The *patch* pocket is a little more casual than either the flap or besom style. It looks exactly like it sounds: a patch of the suit fabric sewn onto the body of the jacket to make a pocket. There may or may not be a flap on it, but if there is, it must never be tucked in.

A sportier version of the patch pocket is one with a center inverted pleat that allows for expansion. This is a very casual touch and is rarely seen on anything but country sports jackets and tweed suits. The presence of the pleat implies that you are actually using the pocket. And the whole idea of the other pocket styles is to put as little in them as possible. Slim lines are the byword, and you can hardly achieve them by stuffing your pockets full of bulky things.

The *bellows* or bag pocket, similar to a patch pocket with a flap, has a piece of pleated fabric attaching it around the sides and bottom to the jacket. Originally used on shooting jackets, it held cartridges and was extremely practical because it expanded without stretching out of shape. Of course bellows pockets are rarely used for this precise purpose today, but they certainly add an air of rusticity to a sports jacket.

As far as trouser pockets are concerned, even here the Peacock Revolution has struck. We say "even here" for the good reason that for decades there were always two very predictable rear pockets: a left one with a button to keep your wallet in place, and on the right, a plain one—an ideal place to keep a functional hand-kerchief. But lately there's been a tendency among some of the more trendy tailors to dispense with rear pockets altogether, which can have a rather disquieting effect on some men. (What these tailors do is to make the front or side pockets much deeper, but it's often not all that practical.) Ergo, if you want those two rear pockets, let your tailor know.

As for the front or side pockets on trousers, there are two main styles: the *slanting* pocket and the *top* pocket. The former tends to bulge at the opening, especially when you're in a seated position, and if overweight is your problem you'd do well to avoid the slanting pocket. (The plainer the pocket the better, should be the overweight man's overall pocket philosophy.) A top pocket has a horizontal slit opening just below the beltline and always stays firmly shut; because of this, it makes for a slimmer silhouette.

Trousers

You'll also have a choice of belt loops with or without buttons for braces—or a waistband sans belt loops and/or buttons. All of which is fodder for some commonsense conversation between you and your tailor. If you decide on belt loops, your next decision must be how deep you want those loops. If they're shallow and you're a wide-belt aficionado—well, you're in for some frustration. But if you prefer your belts on the narrow side (even if the trend is moving in the opposite direction), let your tailor know or he may err in accommodating the wider belt.

So far as cuffs go, remember that cuffs cut height by creating a horizontal effect. The traditionalist invariably chooses a 1½-inch cuff, while many other men prefer more generous cuffs measuring 2 inches or slightly more.

Vest

To be or not to be? That's entirely up to you. If you're lukewarm regarding a vest, why not ask your tailor how much extra a vest adds to the price of the suit. If it's a minimal amount, we suggest you add a vest; it will prove to be the most trouble-free part of the whole tailoring process, even if you're a difficult size to fit. There's always an adjustable strap at the back, and a simple tug at it will spell the difference. (One fashion point: never button the bottom button—not while you're trying it on and not while you're wearing it later.)

One final but very important point regarding your choice of fabric and styling details: Do you want your tailor-made suit to lead a double or even a triple life? In other words, do you want a suit that with a rich-looking shirt and tie will fairly bristle with executive status; with a cashmere turtleneck will look dashing in a discotheque; and whose jacket, with a pair of slacks and a multi-colored sport shirt, will look properly suburban on a weekend? If the answer is Yes, then by all means pass the information on to your friendly tailor and let that guide you both.

Actually, a truly sophisticated tailor will ask you plenty of questions and not take anything for granted, but we suggest you play it safe and volunteer as much pertinent information as possible. A man's relationship with his tailor ought to be as intimate as a woman's with her hairdresser.

HOW TO TAKE CARE OF YOUR SUITS

Hanging

Never keep your suits on wire hangers when they come back from the cleaners; be sure to switch them onto shaped wooden hangers. These approximate the contour of your jacket better and will not pull it out of shape.

When hanging up a suit, take everything out of the pockets, remove the belt from the pants, zip the fly and button the middle button of the jacket. Obviously, all these precautions are taken to prevent undue stress on any part of the suit.

If it's possible, hang the suit where some air can circulate around it. Overcrowded closets are bad in this respect. It's best to hang trousers by special hangers that clamp onto the cuffs, because then there is no bother with the horizontal crease that crossbar hangers can give them.

Brushing

The best policy is to brush the suit after wearing it. There are all kinds of particles that can work their way into the fabric, and they have an abrasive effect that can result in a gradual wearing away of the material. For tweeds, the long-bristled brush is ideal. Smooth-finish fabrics, however, can be "brushed" quite well with adhesive tape. Merely wrap some around your hand a few times, with the sticky side out, and pat your hand over the suit.

Cleaning and Pressing

If you have a dark suit that has permanently creased trousers, it may be difficult for you to determine when you ought to have it cleaned or pressed, or both. Light suits never offer much difficulty; they soil easily and require more cleaning than dark suits do.

As far as pressing is concerned, the trousers may keep their crease, but as you may notice, they can still get a bit baggy after a few wearings. A pressing will restore a sharp line to them, and if it's done on a professional steam iron, this pressing will remove particles of dust from the suit as well (the steam is forced through the fabric, and as a side effect it gives a semicleaning). Suits should be cleaned on an average of once every eight wearings and pressed twice as often.

Naturally this schedule of cleaning varies with the type of climate (hot and sticky: clean more often) and environment (in a city with highly polluted air: clean more often). It's also a good idea to take care of a couple of things that the cleaners never seem to remember. Pull out the pockets and remove dust and lint, and turn down the cuffs and do the same. Also, to augment the cleaning, it's sometimes necessary to rub a cloth with a little cleaning fluid around the edges of the collar. Then when you drop off the suit to be cleaned, be sure to ask that the sleeves be pressed in a rolled manner so that they won't have sharp edges.

Leather buttons and/or leather buckles on your casual suit? Be certain your dry cleaner covers them with foil before cleaning, otherwise there's a very good chance that the process may strip them of color. If the cleaner doesn't do this cover-up job, do it yourself before taking the suit to him.

As for spots and stains, point them out to the dry cleaner and give him some idea of their pedigree since they may require special treatment. And if you'd care to know more on the subject of removing spots and stains without having to turn the garment over to the dry cleaner, we suggest you flip to Chapter Fourteen.

CHAPTER THREE

Shirts and Ties

THE coming of the shaped suit paved the way for the shaped shirt; there simply wasn't any room for a shirt with a excess of material. The tapered shirt with narrower sleeves and lean body lines was the answer, and it slipped into place beneath the shaped jacket.

HOW TO CONFIRM YOUR NECK SIZE AND SLEEVE LENGTH

Now, before you go shopping for your next batch of shirts, we suggest you make sure of your neck and sleeve measurements.

To get your neck size. Slip a tape measure around your neck below the adam's apple. While you hold the tape, swallow; that way you can see how really comfortable a collar that size will be. Read the tape to the nearest half-inch. Should it fall between, for comfort's sake take the higher reading. If the collar's a bit loose, you can fix it by tightening your tie; if it's too small, on the other hand, there's absolutely nothing you can do about it.

To get your sleeve length. Measure from the nape of the neck over the shoulder and down the arm to the tip of the thumb, allowing your arm to bend slightly, as is natural. Now subtract 5 inches from what the tape measures at the tip of the thumb. For instance, if it says 39 inches, your proper shirt sleeve is 34 inches.

FABRICS

We urge you to study the Shirtings Chart in this chapter for all the pithy facts. But we think you should have some additional data on King Cotton, a natural fiber that's been around for at least five thousand years. Cotton was already an old favorite in India and China when one Christopher Columbus noted in his log for October 12, 1492: "They came swimming toward us and brought us parrots, and balls of cotton thread and many other things which they exchanged with us for other things which we gave them such as strings of beads and little bells."

Cotton quality depends on the length of the fiber. Fabrics made from long, thin fibers cost more. *Long-staple cotton* is a superior-quality material because the fibers are longer than most. *Pima cotton* is a high-quality long staple. *Egyptian cotton* is finer and more lustrous than long-staple and pima because of its longer fibers. *Sea Island* and *Supima* cottons are superior to all three because they have extra-long fibers.

Another indication of the quality of cotton fiber is the number of threads woven per inch of fabric. The higher the count, the better the quality of the fabric. High-count cottons are the best.

Knits, of course, have been the big news in dress shirts of the seventies. Like the knit suit, the knit dress shirt is wonderfully comfortable to wear and makes a great traveling shirt. Put it into a suitcase and out it comes fresh and crisp. It's easy to care for, too: most knits (except the woolens) go into a washing machine and dryer and need a minimum of ironing.

Knit dress shirts come in vivid colors and patterns, and often the same shirt does double duty for dress and sportswear. Take one with a spread collar and epaulets; with a tie it's a handsome business shirt, and sans tie it's fair game for a silk ascot and slacks.

Read your label and hangtag carefully, and if you still have any questions regarding the care and feeding of the knit dress shirt you're thinking of buying, consult the salesman.

COLLAR STYLES

The shape of your face should determine the style of your shirt collar. In preparing the following guidelines, we mention some collar styles that may be rarely seen and, in some instances, are in almost total eclipse. Still, any one of them might stage a strong comeback (the button-down, for example, showed strength in the seventies after some seasons of neglect), and for that reason they've been included.

SHIRTINGS CHART

FABRIC	CONTENT	APPEARANCE	WEIGHT	CHARACTERISTICS
BATISTE	Cotton or polyester-cotton blend	Smooth, moderately sheer	Very lightweight (summer)	White and colors
BROADCLOTH	Cotton or polyester-cotton blend	Smooth, faintly ribbed	Medium, year-round	White, colors, patterns; wash-and-wear
DOBBY	Cotton or polyester-cotton blend	Smooth, with small figures	Lightweight	Individual fashion
JACQUARD	Cotton or polyester-cotton blend	Figures, woven on loom with special attachment	Medium	Slightly lustrous
KNIT	Nylon, wool, polyester, Arnel, and any number of blends	Soft hand (soft to handle)	Very lightweight (summer) to medium	Dress, formal and sportswear
LAWN	Cotton	Sheer	Very lightweight (summer)	Mainly white and light colors
LENO	Cotton	Open weave made by pairs of yarns crossing one another	Very lightweight (summer)	Transparent
MADRAS	Cotton	Smooth	Medium	Slightly casual
OXFORD	Cotton or polyester-cotton blend	Roughish texture, woven look	Medium	Slightly casual
PIQUÉ	Cotton	Raised-cord or patterned effect	Medium	Formal
SLUB YARN BROADCLOTH	Cotton or polyester-cotton blend	Nubby	Medium	General purpose
STRETCH BROADCLOTH	Cotton or cotton-polyester plus core-spun (Lycra spandex)	Smooth, slightly ribbed	Medium	Available in white and patterns; has elastic qualities
TRICOT	All polyester or polyester-cotton blend or all nylon	Smooth, finely knitted	Medium	White, solid color or patterned; wash-and-wear

COLLAR STYLES

Regular-medium-point collar	*Medium-point button-down*	*Spread collar*

Long-point button-down	*Rounded-point tab*	*Rounded pin collar*

Round Face

Avoid a tight look around the neck. The button-down collar with regular or long points looks well on you, and for that matter so does any collar with long points. The tab and rounded pin collars are not for you, since they give a balloon effect to a round face by virtue of their own narrowness.

Long, Narrow Face

You're in luck. Practically every collar style is becoming—especially the spread collar. Your only bugaboo: a long pointed collar.

Square Face

The less spread the better. The button-down is your best bet, and the rounded point is also highly flattering. Tip: Avoid too long or too short points.

Oval Face

The rounded collar is your only enemy; it's a case of too much of a good thing—too many smooth curves.

A SHIRT VOCABULARY

Barrel cuff. The basic button-fastened cuff. Newer versions often have several buttons and buttonholes.

Convertible cuff. Has a buttonhole on both ends in addition to a small button, so that it can be buttoned or cuff links can be worn if desired.

The French cuff. Twice the length of the barrel cuff, it is folded back, then held together with cuff links.

Permanent press (also known as durable press). Means the fabric has been chemically treated and heat-cured to give it permanent shape-retaining, wrinkle-shedding properties, as well as flat seams and sharp creases.

Points. The distance from the neckband to the collar's tips.

Sanforized. The best-known finishing treatment for shrink resistance. A shirt so treated will shrink no more than a fraction of one percent.

Slope. The height of the collar on the neck. Usually there's a choice among regular, high or low slope and all collar styles are customarily available in each of these constructions. A high slope makes a long neck seem shorter, while a low slope lengthens a short neck.

Spread. The measurement between the collar tips.

Wash-and-wear. Means the shirting fabric has been resin-coated and heat-treated to make it wrinkle-resistant.

HOW TO TAKE CARE OF YOUR SHIRTS

A starched shirt is passé. A well-made collar, particularly one of a high-quality fabric, will lie neatly without starch. And so far as the life-span of the shirt is concerned, constant starching will cause it to fray easily.

Let your deodorant dry a few seconds before you put your shirt on. Some deodorants while still damp can stain shirting fabrics.

When tying your tie, fold your shirt collar down and slip the tie under it instead of leaving the collar up. This will help keep the collar neat.

Drape a towel around a hanger before putting a wet shirt on it to dry. That way you'll avoid rust and retain collar shape.

Wear a shirt only once between launderings, especially in hot weather. Body oils and dirt can cause collars and cuffs to wear out early.

VARIOUS CLASSES OF TIES

The width of neckwear takes its cue from the suit. A natural shoulder suit with narrow lapels asks for a narrow tie. A shaped suit with wide lapels asks for a wide tie. As ties get wider, fabrics invariably get more opulent; and the thicker the fabric, the larger the knot. So if you have a thin or small face, avoid the very opulent tie fabric or your tie will look like a noose and feel like a ball and chain.

Basically, the most common classes of ties are the following:

Challis. A lightweight, finely spun worsted fabric used in solid-color or printed designs. It's usually tied in a four-in-hand.

Club ties. There are two types, and both are usually made of silk. The first: a solid-color background with a small insignia repeated in diagonal rows. Both the colors and the insignia are those of the club the tie represents. The other type of club tie is like a regimental stripe, no more, no less. And when you get right down to it, the general wearing public has no more idea of what club their club tie belongs to than what regiment their regimental tie belongs to. More important, though, it doesn't matter in either case. In fact, both designs are so widely popular that most club and rep ties floating around have no significance whatever.

Crochet. A knitted-fabric tie, made either by hand or on a machine. The surface is irregular, and it appears in solid colors or stripes. Tied only in four-in-hand.

Faille. A soft, slightly shiny fabric with very fine rib effect. May be made of silk, polyester, rayon or other types of fibers.

Foulard. Twill-weave, lightweight fabric of silk or other fibers, usually in printed figures.

Grenadine. A thin, loosely woven fabric of lightweight silk. It has an irregular surface.

Homespun wool. Loose basket-weave wool, made on a hand loom. Solid colors, stripes or plaids. Occasionally made on a power loom. The tie is thick and is best tied in a four-in-hand knot.

Macclesfield. Rough, open weave, usually in small, compact overall patterns. Used interchangeably with Spitalfields. Names derived from districts in England where they were originally woven.

Mogador. A watered effect on faille or taffeta in solid colors or patterns.

Paisley. Printed or woven designs, adapted to neckwear in foulard, wool or other fabrics from colorful, intricate Kashmirian shawls.

Polka dot. Regularly placed dots on fabric, woven or printed designs. May be white on darker background or colored dots.

Poplin. Fabric woven on grosgrain or ribbed principle, usually silk or polyester with wool filling. Stripes, plaids, solid colors.

Regimental stripes. Looks just like a rep tie, except that the colors and widths of the stripes are those of a British regiment. Few Americans can tell you which is which and most don't know whether they're wearing a regimental or a rep tie.

Rep (repp). Made of a corded fabric with crosswise rib weave and diagonal stripes. Might be made of silk, manmade or other fibers.

Shantung. A fabric woven of irregular yarns, it has a nubby surface and is used in solid colors, stripes or figures. Printed or woven.

FOUR-IN-HAND

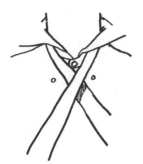

| Cross long end over short end | Bring long end under short end | Bring long end around short end |

| Bring long end through center at top | Pull long end through loop and form center crease | Slide completed knot into place |

Shepherd's check. Small, even checks in contrasting colors. May be in twill silk, wool or blends of fibers.

HOW TO TIE ONE ON

Four-in-Hand

The ideal knot for wide ties of heavy fabrics and wide knits.

Windsor

Once dear to the hearts of fashionables on both sides of the Atlantic, this luxurious knot went out of favor for the good reason that a very wide tie makes a wide knot, so who needs a wide

WINDSOR

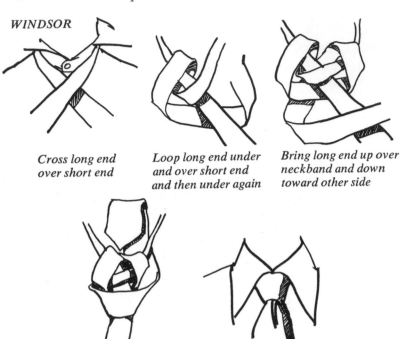

Cross long end
over short end

Loop long end under
and over short end
and then under again

Bring long end up over
neckband and down
toward other side

Wrap long end around front of
knot, then loop it under neckband
and down through loop

Slide completed
knot into place

Windsor knot? But although the Windsor is *morte* during the era of the wide tie, you ought to know how to tie one on Windsor-fashion, for it will make a comeback if the narrow tie does.

Half Windsor

A happy compromise, it incorporates more fabric into the knot but the result isn't as bulky as the Windsor. Still, it's recommended only for wide ties with lightweight fabrics that aren't heavily lined.

1. Start with the wide end on your right, hanging about a foot below the narrow end.

2. Cross the wide end over the narrow, then turn it back underneath.

3. Bring it up over the neckband and down through the opposite side.

4. Pass it around the front, from left to right.

5. Take it up underneath through the neckband.

6. Finally, pass it down through the knot in front. Tighten it carefully—not too tight—and draw it up to the collar.

Bow

The late 1960s witnessed the return of the bow tie in a very wide style called a *kipper*. Be wary of the very wide bow tie since it has the effect of all but devouring the thin face and blowing up the full face. There are bows in every size and shape (butterfly, bat, et cetera), so you have only to experiment before a mirror to find your best bet. (Although the pre-tied bow is acceptable today for even the most formal occasions, the purist maintains that only the hand-tied bow has status.)

1. Start with both ends of the tie hanging evenly.

2. Slide the left end down until it hangs about 1½ inches below the right end.

3. Cross the long end over the short and pass it underneath the loop that has developed.

4. Double up the short end and place it across the collar points, centered approximately where the knot will be.

5. Hold it there with the thumb and forefinger of the left hand and drop the long end down over the front.

6. Place the right forefinger, pointing up, on the bottom half of the hanging part; then pass it up underneath the loop formed by the short end.

7. Another loop has been formed, which you poke through the knot behind the front loop.

8. Tug, twist, even up until both ends are as wide as the spread of your eyes.

Sport Ascot

A decidedly breezy touch for a sports outfit, and very simple to tie:

Just a single knot, held for convenience by a pin through the knot and hidden by the draped end.

HOW TO TAKE CARE OF YOUR TIES

Hang them on a tie rack. Ties have a tendency to slide and twist on a hanger.

Stains are best removed with cleaning fluid (but test it on the inside of the tie first). Overall cleaning and pressing, however, should always be entrusted to a topnotch dry cleaner.

Rub your fingertips on a towel before putting on your tie; even the slightest hint of body oil can stain a tie fabric, especially the silks.

Never tie a knot too tight. Ties that are knotted too tightly lose their shape quickly.

Knit ties stretch. Never hang them; instead roll them and store in a drawer.

Give your ties a chance to "breathe." Give them a few days' rest between wearings.

Never leave a tie permanently knotted.

Always unknot your tie by reversing the tying process. Loosening it and slipping it over your head puts unnecessary stress on the tie.

CHAPTER FOUR

Color and Pattern
Coordination

I T's difficult to believe that until the Prince of Wales sported a bright red tie back in the 1920s, such a tie was off limits to any man who prized his reputation as a virile male animal. Today colors have no gender and a lush shade of peach or plum is as much at home in *his* wardrobe as in *her* wardrobe. Still, color can be a tricky ally and a few basic pointers should be recognized before a man feels color-secure enough to experiment. And so the following guidelines are not meant to inhibit you but instead to give you enough self-confidence to be more colorful.

THE BLUE SUIT

Without question, the blue suit is the easiest color to wear, which undoubtedly explains why, since the "invention" of the suit as we know it, a blue suit has been a staple in most men's wardrobes. Blue is an exceptionally flattering color for blond-, gray- and white-haired men, particularly in the medium to dark shades. If your hair is brown or black, any shade of blue is becoming. Even the redhead has no real problem with a blue suit, although his best bets are browns and grays.

Shirt

Few color restrictions here, since almost any color except tan goes well with blue. Say, white . . . blue . . . gray . . . pink . . . yellow . . . red stripes. Green? Only a green with a grayish cast will work, and even that isn't anywhere near as attractive as those shirt colors we've just ticked off.

54

Tie

Again, steer clear of tan or brown unless combined with blue, and even then it's not likely to be all that attractive. And why bother when you can get such great effects with the following tie colors: red, maroon, blue, light gray, ivory, gold? Eschew the all-black or all-green tie, though green and black as accents in stripes or pattern interest work well.

Pocket Handkerchief

White and colored handkerchiefs that relate to the colors in the shirt or tie.

THE GRAY SUIT

It's most flattering to men with black hair, but really any man can wear a gray suit. The blond-, gray- or white-haired gent should choose a suit in medium to darker shades of gray. Brown- or red-haired men can wear any shade, and so can men with ruddy or tanned complexions. But if you have a fair or pale complexion, you'd do well to wear a medium to darker shade.

Shirt

White . . . blue . . . pale yellow . . . pale olive . . . pink. A gray shirt only if it's lighter than the suit and offers contrast. A tan shirt is possible but tricky to coordinate.

Tie

You can really play the field here, ruling out only a solid gray tie of the same tonality as your suit.

Pocket Handkerchief

White is safe but dull when paired with most gray suits. Try blue, red, black, gold, maroon, a shade of gray different from that of your suit—by themselves or in pattern combinations and coordinated with your shirt and tie colors.

THE BROWN SUIT

When we say brown we mean everything from the tan or so-called natural-color suit to the charcoal brown suit.

The man with a ruddy or tanned complexion can wear any shade of brown. And so can the man with brown hair. Blonds, on the other hand, are better off with the medium to darker shades, although a tan suit that has a grayish cast is very flattering to their fair coloring. The sallow-skinned should also favor this cooler shade of tan, taking care to avoid all the golden browns. Redheads do best with browns that don't have too much red in them, and charcoal brown is an A-1 choice for the man with black hair, as well as most men with a gray or white thatch. But let's end on this more positive note: the camel-color suit is a warm, neutral tan shade any man can wear.

Shirt

White . . . tan . . . yellow . . . pale olive . . . true green. If your brown suit is a gray-brown, go for the pink and red stripes. Light gray and blue shirts work well with brown suits. With the tan suit, wear shirts in soft shades of pink, blue or green; a beige shirt in a tone lighter or deeper than your tan suit adds up to a tone-on-tone look that is especially rich.

Tie

Dark brown ties look great with suits in the lighter shades of brown, while tan and ivory ties complement the darker shades of brown. Green, gray, olive and gold are all handsome tie colors with a brown suit. And blue ties can go with brown suits that have a blue or gray cast. But a brown suit with even a trace of green in it can't take a red tie; a maroon tie, however, looks handsome with a brown suit that has an olive cast. Solid-black knits and black and white ties are fine fashion companions for the tan suit. A particularly dashing shirt and tie combination with tan is a pale pink shirt and a dark red tie. With the very versatile camel shade, a navy blue tie is another dandy choice—whether a solid color or a navy and white stripe or polka dot—and so is gray in any shade from silver down to charcoal.

Pocket Handkerchief

White or colored handkerchiefs that relate to the colors in the shirt or tie. With the lighter shades of brown, forget the white handkerchief and choose one that picks up the strongest color in your shirt or tie.

THE GREEN SUIT

There was a time when few men dared a green suit. But today there are so many attractive shades of green available, there is at least one shade for every man. Still, some men are a little green when it comes to wearing green and so we decided it would be wise to deal individually with each of the four most popular shades:

Loden

This is the flattering gray-green that came to us via the Austrian Tyrol. Any man can wear it because it's subtle and adapts itself to any number of shirt and tie color combinations. The loden green suit is most attractive with shirts of clear yellow, bone, pale green, light blue, gray-blue, white and ivory. You can afford to go stronger with your ties: dark blues, dark greens and the dark reds like brick, claret and burgundy.

Pine Green

Or Christmas tree green. The redhead with the very fair complexion should steer clear of this one since it tends to wash him out. Best shirt colors are clear yellow, lemon yellow, tan, beige, ivory, white, gingham checks in two contrasting shades of green, and any shirt boasting stripes of pink and white or strawberry and white. As for ties, choose a darker-than-pine green solid color or a green and white or green and' red striped tie. Also extremely attractive are the clear blues, dark golds (antique to mustard) and the clear bright reds, as well as those darker reds we listed for the loden green suits.

Hunter Green

This is one of the darker-than-pine greens we were referring to above, and it's possibly the most popular of all the greens. If you have a sallow complexion, hunter green is your fashion ally (so long as you avoid yellow accessories). And it's also very flattering to men with gray or white hair. The most attractive shirt colors with this shade of green suit are those listed for pine green. And the same holds true when it comes to tie colors, except that where the pine green suit calls for a darker shade of green, the hunter green suit calls for a lighter shade of green.

Olive

This is often the green that first won many a man over to the green family, mainly because olive comes in such a wide variety of tones. And since the choice is so wide, men with blond, gray or white hair would be wise to avoid the lighter tones of olive. And unfortunately, there isn't any tone of olive that looks good on the man with a sallow complexion; as already noted, hunter green is his green. White, yellow, green, pink, mauve, rust, gray, tan, olive, red and white stripes, and tattersall checks in yellow and brown, red and green, and blue and black add up to sensational shirts with any olive suit. And while the blue shirt may not sound compatible with olive, it is if the suit is of a blue-olive mixture. Ties of yellow, green, brown, gold, tan, gray, rust, pimento red and maroon are all good choices. And so is the medium to dark blue tie when worn with the olive suit that has some blue in it.

What about the pocket handkerchief for your green suit? White looks crisp with the medium and darker shades but since green is such a fresh suit color, why not strive for some color contrast that is a spin-off from one of the colors in your shirt or tie?

PATTERNS

The pattern-on-pattern approach is a sure sign of today's fashion freedom. A combination that was once taboo—say, a merry mix of checks and plaids in suit, tie and shirt—is now the sign of the more sophisticated dresser. Turnbull & Asser in London, one of the world's most civilized menswear emporiums, will feature a checked jacket worn with glen plaid trousers and only the most tradition-bound peer will pop his monocle at the sight. But let's face facts: it takes plenty of taste and know-how to achieve this brand of throwaway chic.

A handy rule: one strong, one soft, one unifying pattern. There are, you see, degrees of pattern strength. For instance, there's a whopping big difference between muted checked shirts and bold black checked shirts—and between ties with minute yellow polka dots on a navy background and those with giant yellow polka dots on a navy background. Furthermore, color also affects pattern. A shirt striped in light gray or blue can naturally carry more pattern in a tie than a shirt striped in bright red or hot pink. And never forget that your suit is the springboard from which you start. Beyond that, keep an open mind and conquer any prerevolutionary inhibitions that may still be lurking in the corners of your psyche.

Now, to get you thinking positively, here are some really first-rate marriages of patterns with patterns:

A glen plaid suit with an overcheck; generally patterned tie; striped shirt.

A box plaid suit; floral jacquard tie; tone-on-tone checked shirt.

A big windowpane check suit; paisley silk tie; chevron-striped shirt.

A giant herringbone-patterned suit; geometric print tie; multistriped shirt.

A chalk plaid patterned suit; a silk pin-dot tie; a pinstripe shirt picking up the dominant color of the suit and alternating it with white.

A textured herringbone suit; antique floral brocaded tapestry tie; a woven jacquard striped shirt with harmonized solid collar and cuffs.

A windowpane plaid suit; checked shirt; geometric-motif tie.

Get the idea? Be brave and experiment. But before you start on the adventure of mixing patterns, study the following Pattern Coordination Chart.

PATTERN COORDINATION CHART

SUIT	SHIRT	TIE	
HERRINGBONE OR DIAGONAL WEAVE	Solid color	Solid color Narrow or wide stripes Small allover figures	Bold patterns Checks and plaids
	Striped*	Solid color Wide stripe Small allover figures	Bold patterns Checks and plaids
	Checked	Solid color	Wide stripe
PRONOUNCED PLAID	Solid color	Solid color Under-the-knot designs Panel designs	Narrow or wide stripes Small allover figures Polka dots
	Striped*	Solid color Under-the-knot designs Panel designs	Wide stripes Small allover figures Polka dots
	Checked	Solid color	Under-the-knot designs
CHECKED OR MINIATURE PLAID	Solid color	Solid color Under-the-knot designs Panel designs Narrow or wide stripes	Small allover figures Bold patterns Subtle polka dots

PATTERN COORDINATION CHART (*cont'd*)

SUIT	SHIRT	TIE	
	Striped*	Solid color Under-the-knot designs Panel designs Wide stripes	Small allover figures Bold patterns Subtle polka dots
SOLID COLOR (INCLUDING SELF-WEAVE EFFECTS THAT GIVE THE IMPRESSION OF A SOLID)	Solid color	Anything except solid color	
	Striped*	Anything except stripes of same width	
	Checked	Solid color Under-the-knot designs	Panel designs Wide stripes
STRIPED	Solid color	Anything	
	Striped* (muted if suit stripe is strong and vice versa)	Anything except stripes	
CHECKED	Panel designs Wide stripes	Solid color Under-the-knot designs	

*We refer here to finely striped shirts; with wide, bolder stripes in shirtings, ties should be solid color, under-the-knot or carefully selected panel designs or allover figures.

CHAPTER FIVE

Shoes and Socks

Footwear, like every other important article of apparel, takes its fashion cue from the suit. The shaped suit with wide lapels and flared trousers ushered in a look of "more shoe" along with wider ties and spread-collar shirts, just as the natural shoulder suit of the fifties with its straight-hanging lines brought on the trimmer, lighter-weight shoe along with narrow ties and button-down shirts. Suit silhouettes will continue to change and so, too, will shoes. No one can predict how they'll change; the only safe prediction is that they will. But one thing is certain: gone is the day when a well-polished, freshly soled oxford was all that was expected of a well-shod man. Today's shoes are as fashionable as they are functional. And we think *Esquire* expressed the contemporary attitude toward footwear when it noted: "Of all items in the male wardrobe, shoes unquestionably express a man's vanity at its most indulgent."

HOW TO SHOP FOR A NEW PAIR OF SHOES

There's a lot of ground to be covered here, so we'll start at the very beginning and give you a few salient pointers on how to prepare to shop for a new pair of shoes:

1. Shop for shoes in midafternoon. Why? Because by that time you've been on your feet and walking around long enough to allow your feet to spread to their daily maximum. This is the very best way to guarantee the proper fit.

2. Try to wear a shoe style very like the style you're planning to buy. Slip-ons, for instance, permit feet to spread or swell. This then will cause some confusion when trying on a pair of laced

shoes, which naturally fit closer and don't allow for the same sort of expansion.

3. Always wear the same thickness of sock you expect to be wearing when you use the shoe. Still another way of guaranteeing proper fit.

4. When trying on the new shoe, bend its toe gently but firmly to loosen it. Also work the rim of the heel with your palm in the same manner.

5. Walk the length and breadth of the shoe store or shoe department to get some indication of how comfortable these new shoes will be, but face the fact that this is never really more than a sixty-second workout at best. So what you should do is this: choose your shoes, then take them home and really try them out. (Always, of course, in a carpeted area so that the sole isn't scuffed.) Wear them for an entire evening. We guarantee that if you do this two evenings in a row, you'll know for certain whether these are the shoes for you or not. And if they're not, they'll still look good as new and you'll be able to effect an exchange.

A FOOTWEAR VOCABULARY

Bal. This is the best-known fastening in men's shoes. It has a V construction that starts at the top of the vamp and features a series of eyelets through which the shoelaces are threaded.

Gore. An essential part of the slip-on style shoe, gores are the pieces of elastic material inserted into the sides which allow the foot to slide in more easily. In some slip-ons the gores are concealed inside the shoe but more and more they've become part of the design.

Oxford. This name applies to any footwear style that extends no farther than the ankle. A heavy oxford is called a *brogue.*

Sole. And from the standpoint of upkeep, it might be spelled *soul.* At any rate, it's the bottom of the shoe and, depending on the shoe it's attached to, can be either smooth or textured. Made from leather, rubber and synthetic materials, or cork for more casual footwear.

Vamp. The section of the shoe that lies between the toe and the instep.

THE LEATHERS

Buckskin. A particularly soft, velvety leather with a suedelike finish. The all-white and the brown buckskin shoe for casual wear came to the fore back in the twenties; the brown buck was given an enormous boost by the Prince of Wales' penchant for the cocoa brown buckskin shoe during his visit to the U.S. in 1923.

Calfskin. A supple leather with a smoother appearance because it is, as the name suggests, taken from calves and therefore is a younger, more elastic leather. (Which is why calfskin shoes cost more.)

Cordovan. A tough, smooth leather taken from the hindquarters of a horse. On the plus side, cordovan is very scuff-resistant and polishes to a high gloss. On the minus side, cordovan shoes can give some men a "hot foot," since this leather is not porous. The legendary Man in the Gray Flannel Suit of the 1950s liked to wear cordovans with his charcoal gray suit, pink button-down shirt and narrow black knit tie.

Patent leather. This is leather that has been coated to give it a permanent, extraordinarily shiny finish. Patent leather, long associated with black shoes for formal and semiformal occasions, has in the past few years taken to the streets for daytime wear in both brown and white—the latter making a particularly stylish sport shoe. It was once considered very impractical except for special-occasion wear since it was prone to wrinkle and crack, but today's patent leathers are much more supple and durable.

Side leather. The leather most often used for shoes because while it's tough and durable, it's also lightweight and supple—a combination of traits that helps it translate into any number of shapes, patterns and textures.

Suede. Actually this is not a leather but rather a finish; any leather can be turned into suede by brushing the underside of the skin with a rough surface to bring up its nap. The most expensive suede shoes are those made of calfskin.

CLASSIC SHOE STYLES

The following are capsule descriptions of the most classic shoe styles. Naturally, there are variations of these classics—as well as variations of the variations—but the following are the big daddies from which all others spin off:

Plain-toe blucher (the blucher effect is the curvature at the bottom of the eyelet stays over the instep). This is a five-eyelet model. A particularly serviceable shoe in black, brown, cordovan and all white.

Moccasin slip-on. This style has a strap over the instep and is otherwise known as the *loafer.* It is a descendant of the original style of moccasin slip-ons introduced in the 1930s. Available in smooth, grained and brushed surface materials.

Moccasin-style oxford. These shoes are identifiable by the parabolas of stitching around the upper. A four-eyelet blucher front.

Slip-on with low-set hand-stitched border. Quite plainly developed from the loafer, it is somewhat more dressy.

Three-eyelet shoe with low-set stitching. Ditto the above. And like the above, can be worn for sports or for business.

Saddle-strap shoe in all brown, all black or all white. Also available in white with brown or black saddle straps. A casual type of shoe that was a rage in the thirties, the saddle shoe made a strong comeback in the early seventies on the golf links.

Full brogue wing tip. This is a thick, heavy shoe; a traditional style. In smooth- or grained-textured materials, with blucher front, perforated-design toe cap, sturdy soles, and often with a welt seam around the edge.

Plain-toe slip-on shoe. Depending on the leather, it's appropriate for business, sports and formal evening wear.

Boot. Any footwear that extends higher than the top of the ankle.

Demiboot. A short boot measuring anywhere from 6 inches (slightly above the ankle) to 10 inches (midcalf).

Two-eyelet chukka boot. A high blucher with soles made of leather, rubber or composition. Really the first boot to win universal acceptance.

SHOES

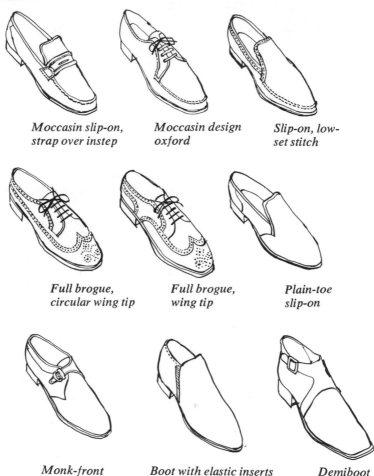

| Moccasin slip-on, strap over instep | Moccasin design oxford | Slip-on, low-set stitch |

| Full brogue, circular wing tip | Full brogue, wing tip | Plain-toe slip-on |

| Monk-front | Boot with elastic inserts | Demiboot |

Ghillie. A shoe that has leather loops instead of eyelets, a motif derived from the heavy shoes worn in nineteenth-century Scotland and revived in the 1960s via lightweight models and boots.

Fringe-tongue golf shoe with moccasin design. The fringe is sometimes called "kilt tongue." It's seen in black, brown, all white or combinations of black and white, and brown and white.

Monk-front shoe (with strap-and-buckle closure over the instep

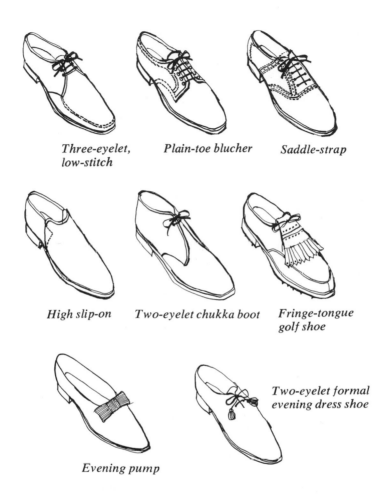

Three-eyelet, low-stitch   *Plain-toe blucher*   *Saddle-strap*

High slip-on   *Two-eyelet chukka boot*   *Fringe-tongue golf shoe*

Two-eyelet formal evening dress shoe

Evening pump

and perfectly plain tip). In plain black, brown or all white, this British import became one of the most popular styles of the early seventies.

Evening pump. For wear with tuxedo or white tie. Most often in patent leather, it has very lightweight soles, and a dull, ribbed grosgrain ribbon.

Two-eyelet formal evening dress shoe. In black lustrous material.

Good for wear with dinner jacket or tailcoat. Five-eyelet versions of this shoe are generally worn only with black tie.

FOOTWEAR FASHION GUIDELINES

Two-toned and two-textured shoes, and higher heels (some up to 2 inches), will go down in fashion's history books as characteristic of the early seventies, a sure sign that footwear had caught up with the rest of men's liberated fashions. How far you care to travel that road to self-expression is of course entirely up to you, but the day when a salesman looked up at you from his fitting stool and queried, "Black or brown?" is ancient history. And so far as rules go, they're made for breaking. After all, back in the early sixties many a blue chip corporation frowned on their men wearing tasseled moccasins, while today a patent leather slip-on sporting a metal chain or a pair of demiboots is seen in even the most conservative business offices.

There are, however, still a few guidelines:

1. Save your more colorful footwear for your casual clothes. They clash with a business-suit-tie-and-shirt outfit.

2. A rounded or blunted toe makes a foot appear smaller. So if you're a short man with small feet, choose something somewhat more pointed. (But the exaggerated pointed toe is passé.)

3. If you're a tall, thin man steer clear of a very pointed toe no matter how modish it may be at the time. And of course the higher heel is not for you.

4. Boots are not for every man; certainly not for the short man, who must confine himself to the demiboot.

5. Fashionable men started mixing brown shoes with blue and gray suits, and black shoes with brown suits, way back in the elegant thirties. Still, every shade of brown doesn't go with a blue suit, no more than any shade of black can take on a brown suit. Black suits have such an emphatic personality you will find the best brown shoes to wear with them are also extremes. For example, black suits look particularly elegant with the dark brown shoe that is so dark it's the closest you can get to black and still remain in the brown family. With the summer-weight black suits more

freedom is permitted. They look particularly well with shoes of that special tan sand color.

HOW TO TAKE CARE OF YOUR SHOES

Shine 'em before you wear 'em. That should be your motto with every pair of shoes you buy. They'll be that much easier to shine as time goes on, and furthermore they won't scuff so easily.

Always use a shoehorn, otherwise you'll permanently crinkle the back of the shoe.

Give your shoes a rest. In other words, don't wear the same pair two days in a row. That way the shoe interiors will stay fresher and the shoes will stay younger-looking longer, inside and outside.

Have a pair of shoe trees for every pair of shoes you own. Inexpensive metal or plastic ones—the kind you can buy at what used to be called a five-and-ten-cent store—will do just fine. Trees help shoes retain their shape.

When shoes have sloshed through the rain or snow, never dry them out by a radiator. Best treatment for damp shoes is to insert shoe trees . . . brush off accumulated dirt and grime from top and bottom . . . and when they're dry, apply a leather preservative to restore the luster of the leather.

Keep your shoes well heeled. Run-down heels not only look pathetic but they also affect the balance and shape of the shoe by straining the joints and seams.

Never use petroleum jelly on patent leather shoes; it will gum them up and haze over the shine. Instead invest in one of the special patent leather cleaners that clean, polish, soften and preserve patents of all colors. In lieu of a special cleaner, wipe them first with a damp cloth, then a dry one; or apply a furniture spray and wipe off.

Suede shoes deserve their own brush, a stiff-bristled job that brings up the nap while it whisks off the dirt and dust. Wet suedes should be brushed lightly just as soon as they're dry.

Metal taps affixed to the front underside of each shoe will protect the fronts from wearing out prematurely. And rubber taps will prolong the life-span of heels.

SOCKS: A FASHION ACCESSORY

Until the Peacock Revolution, patterned socks were relegated to weekend wear with country tweeds and corduroys. Socks for business wear were almost always exclusively dark, whatever the color: brown, gray, wine, blue or green. Clocks (remember them?) were about the only decoration men were permitted.

Today, however, socks are truly a fashion accessory—an accent that sparks the wardrobe—and the free-spirited patterns and uninhibited colors once relegated to casual socks are now being worn with business suits.

Wool and nylon arc the two best-known sock materials, and then there are the ribbed lisles (a high-quality cotton yarn) and such synthetics as polyester and acrylic fibers. The synthetics, however, simply aren't as absorbent as cotton or wool socks unless, of course, they're antistatic socks.

The *antistatic* sock is one of the most newsworthy innovations; it means that the sock won't collect lint or have your trouser legs clinging to your socks. This is accomplished via a treatment developed for synthetic materials, and a not inconsiderable side benefit of this treatment is the fact that it also makes synthetic hosiery fabric more absorbent and thereby cooler. Antron III is an antistatic nylon fabric. But the treatment is known as Endo-Stat and when you see this on a label or hangtag it means that the sock is of an antistatic synthetic fabric.

A SOCKS VOCABULARY

Argyles. Popular knit design consisting of diamond shapes, usually alternating in three colors.

Athletic socks (or crew socks). Anklet length, thickly ribbed white socks sporting some sort of striped band near or at the top.

Boot. The portion of the sock that fits over the leg, from the top to the base of the heels.

Cushioned foot. A looped or terry stitch on the inner sole of the sock made with an additional yarn.

Heathers. Multicolor effects produced by using two or more colors or yarns twisted together.

Links-and-links. Textured weaves such as basket weaves, cables, et cetera, which may be used in side panels or throughout the sock.

Rib. An alternating raised and lowered surface on a sock.

Stretch. The secret behind the one-size-fits-all sock. More specifically, it is the name for the expandable texture filament or polyester yarn that is specially treated to give it the characteristics of a coil spring.

Support socks. Elastic fibers knitted into the hose provide the legs with firm support.

SOCKS FASHION GUIDELINES

For decades the liveliest socks with the most personality were seen on the golf links, in full view since most golfers wore knickers. But fashion being the perverse devil it is, today's golfer wears slacks and one rarely gets a peek at his socks. On the other hand, the argyles and other lively-patterned socks are now being worn with business suits. And that's how it goes. One thing remains constant, however: *over-the-calf* is the only length sock you wear with a suit.

Since this is a pattern-on-pattern fashion era we live in, don't be timid about wearing patterned socks. But when you're really dabbling in patterns (a herringbone suit with checkered shirt and wide striped tie, for instance), solid-color socks make good fashion sense. The contrast will work for you.

Bear in mind that the size and color of the pattern of your hosiery have much to do with its suitability for your suit. In short, the suit should wear the sock—the accessory—and not vice versa. Whenever you're in serious doubt, slip on a pair of solid-color socks; you won't be copping out—not with all the luscious shades that are around today.

HOW TO TAKE CARE OF YOUR SOCKS

Easy. Socks may be either hand washed or machine washed. When washed and dried, turn socks inside out to prevent lint. Use hot water for synthetics; warm water for cotton or wool.

CHAPTER SIX

Outerwear

W HEN you come right down to it, there are only a few months of the year when you're not covered up with those items of apparel that come under the heading of Outerwear. And in view of this fact, your outerwear should make as positive a fashion statement as your shaped suit.

OVERCOATS AND TOPCOATS

Someone once observed that there is never a time when men's apparel isn't touched by the elegance of other eras. This is being proved especially true with our contemporary outercoats, for updated versions of old favorites are rife, although the modern renderings often have little more than a nodding acquaintance with the original. Still, a new interpretation of a fashion classic makes great good sense, being based on a tried and true fashion rather than a passing fad. And when you're paying a substantial price for an outercoat, this is indeed a point in its favor.

Among some of the all-time popular coats, you'll find several that recall earlier decades:

The Camel's Hair Coat

Camel's hair is a lightweight, soft and comfortably warm wool, and its blond-tan shade is immensely flattering. Certainly no coat in the 1920s and 1930s had the fashion clout of the camel's hair polo coat, popularized by Ivy League undergraduates. They had picked it up from members of a visiting British polo team who liked to sit around between plays with these sporty coats tossed casually over their shoulders. The classic polo coat was a six-button double-breasted model with half belt, but soon there were single-breasted box styles, four-button models with raglan shoulders and all-around belts, and even wraparounds with no buttons and a tied belt.

Now the camel-shaded coat is in vogue again, in all sorts of guises and any number of fabrics as well as camel's hair. These contemporary versions run the gamut from eight-button double-breasteds to buttonless wraparounds.

The British Warm

Another classic of the camel's hair polo coat era, it is a subtly shaped and dressy double-breasted coat that traces its origin back to the taupe-color World War I British officer's coat. It has made its comeback with all its styling features virtually intact; the one notable bit of updating is the placement of the two flapped pockets down at the level of the bottom row of buttons, where they've been tilted at a particularly sharp slant. Some but not all of the current British warms still carry their shoulder epaulets.

This is a particularly flattering overcoat style for most men and comes in a variety of fabrics, such as the original British warm's melton cloth (one of the most serviceable cloths for outerwear); cashmere, a very fine soft wool (and one of the most luxurious and costly); and cavalry twill, a tough hard-finish worsted with a steep diagonal rib design.

The Long, Shaped Coat

Produced in both overcoat and topcoat fabrics, these midi- and maxi-length coats feature hefty lapels, generous pockets and usually a fair amount of flare at the bottom. There are solid colors, bold chalk stripes and every conceivable pattern. Denim and suede, two fabrics once restricted to sportswear apparel, are particularly popular in this style of coat. Some versions, featuring high waists and plenty of brass buttons, look as if they've stepped out of the Napoleonic wars. (You'll notice that buttons have taken on genuine fashion status; fly-front closures are rarely seen except in rainwear.)

The Leather Coat

The last time this great revival was around in quantity it was considered strictly for sportswear. Nowadays a leather coat is acceptable in the city, and a leather trench coat or a leather coat with fur trim ranks high on the fashion chart.

The Wraparound Coat

This enjoyed a limited popularity back in the twenties and thirties, and now has staged a strong comeback in every length from well above the knee to well below the knee. Buttonless, with wide lapels, a generous collar and a sash belt, it comes in all shades of solid colors and patterns and is especially effective in fleecy wool, cashmere or vicuña, the aristocrat of fabrics. This is a sporty coat, looking best with a turtleneck sweater or a loosely tied ascot scarf, and if your wardrobe is a limited one, you'd be wise to consider a more traditional coat style.

FUR COATS

At the turn of this century, when winters were *winters,* affluent gentlemen were sporting double-breasted fur and fur-lined coats. And of course the raccoon coat was in every fashionable man's wardrobe during the twenties. But the fur coat faded from the scene with the depression thirties and didn't stage a comeback until the late fifties, when fur hats imported from Sweden started making American men fur-conscious all over again. In 1958, for instance, *Esquire* was trumpeting: "They're all yours, men—fur coats, fur collars, fur hats!" adding this historical footnote: "In medieval Europe fur was almost exclusively a male prerogative."

Today fur coats for men are no longer for the daring few. Some are genuine fur and some are amazing look-alikes in synthetic fibers that cost less and also ease the conscience of the ecologically oriented individual. (You can pick up a black mink for about $3,500, or a fake mink for under $200. Minks, by the way, are bred solely for fur and are therefore what is known as a nonendangered species.)

Fur coat lengths go from above the knee down to the maxi length, and there is quite literally a fur for every occasion: for country, a cardigan sweater style; for sport, a ski parka; for après-sport, a hip-length model; for leisure, a pea jacket style. Why, you can even have a fur trench coat with leather trim. In short, just about any style outercoat you can have in fabric, you can now have in fur, genuine or fake.

GLOVES

Probably the only article of wearing apparel with a belligerent history is the glove. Gallant men used to fling it down with gusto as a symbol of challenge, or perhaps swat another's face with it for the ultimate insult. Now the glove is important for two other reasons: warmth and fashion. It's the second of these that concerns us here.

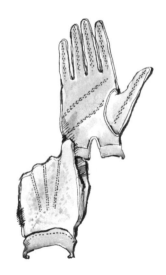

Basic Varieties

Pigskin. Primarily in natural tan or cork shades, but also seen in dark brown or gray.

Mocha. A sueded-finish leather in soft shades of gray, brown, olive or black. This is a luxuriant glove and has a dressier look than pigskin.

Smooth leathers. Such as capeskin and deerskin. Available in a variety of colors.

Rough-surfaced leathers. Buckskin, for example. The appearance is sporty and rugged, and the gloves are worn accordingly.

The outside design of gloves is fairly limited, as you might imagine. Since all models end up "fitting like a glove," there is little basic difference among them. The few variants that do exist, such as stitching and vents (some are on the side, others are but a slit at the center underside), are of virtually no significance.

The inside treatment is another story. A glove, since it is intended to keep the hands warm, can be lined. Linings can be of knitted wool, luxurious cashmere or fine soft fur. Which it is to be is solely a personal matter for the wearer to decide. Fashion, at this point, has little relevance; comfort is the only guide.

Specialty Models

Besides "dress" gloves, there are a number of specialty models. Skiers, for example, favor fur-lined gloves, quilted leather gloves, leather-palmed fabric knits, and fur or quilted mittens.

Leather and knitted combinations originated with the horseback rider. The fabric back provides aeration while the leather palm affords a good grip and effective protection for the hands against chafing on the reins. The same principle holds true for driving an automobile. Leather palms are essential for the steering wheel, because knits would slip and make driving hazardous. And speaking of aeration, there are two-toned leather driving gloves featuring cutouts for a snappy "seminude" look.

Golf and archery gloves are really more "equipment" than gloves. Both have sliced-off fingers and are worn without regard to warmth or fashion.

Every year there is an average of 122 rainy days in twenty-eight of the largest American cities. While that certainly doesn't make us sound as soggy as London or Dublin, it's soggy enough to suggest you should be prepared to protect your handsome threads with something worthy of them. And you'll have only yourself to blame if you don't, since never before has rainwear offered such a variety of lengths, styles and fabrics.

Raincoats

Before we get to our rundown on what's out there waiting to be bought, let's do our rainy-day homework and clear up any foggy notions you may have regarding waterproof and water-repellent.

When a fabric is *waterproofed*, it is coated with rubber, linseed oil, neoprene or a comparable substance. Once this coating process meant closing the pores of the fabric completely, but no more. Today a fabric can be waterproofed and at the same time remain porous enough to allow the passage of air through the cloth.

A fabric becomes *water-repellent* via a finishing process based on resins, plastics, waxes or emulsions. These are used to impregnate the cloth, which is then cured and heat-set. Once such a cloth had to be treated again after every cleaning, but now a fabric can be made permanently water-repellent.

All of which comes down to this: a waterproofed garment will hold out water if submerged in it; a water-repellent fabric sheds water but will leak eventually if submerged.

Of course, no discussion of raincoats would be worthwhile if it first didn't tip the umbrella in the direction of the *trench coat,* the father of them all. The fashion impact of the trench coat, for instance, is chiefly responsible for the fact that the most popular raincoat styles are traditionally those with a military look.

This swashbuckler of a coat came out of the trenches of the First World War, where it had served as an all-weather coat for the doughboys, its fine twill cotton gabardine fabric having been chemically processed to repel rain. In the war years the trench coat

TRENCH COAT

had been a four-button double-breasted style with shoulder or gun flaps, straps on the sleeves, an all-around belt with brass rings (to hold a water bottle and hand grenades), a convertible collar and a deep vent with an inset of fabric fastened with a button. The coat had a buttoned-in lining of wool with sleeves, and even this lining was interlined with an oiled fabric.

Not surprisingly, the trench coat was a fantastic success as a military coat and went on to rack up a civilian success story that by now is legendary. Some of the heroic proportions of the trench coat have been streamlined over the years (reduced shoulder flaps, sometimes a half belt), but its dashing personality is still intact, and no man is out of fashion who sports one, whether it be in an off-white or sand shade, or black, navy, olive or one of the many deep browns.

The classic raincoat fabrics are cotton poplin or twill; the blend of polyester and cotton fibers appears in twills as well as poplin weaves. Blends of polyester and wool are usually reserved for coats carrying a bit more weight, and the all-wool worsted is seen mainly in gabardines and more pronounced twills. Newer rainwear fabrics include denim, cotton canvas and the knits (of course).

A double-knit trench coat or variation of the trench coat is available, and if you happen to be one of those men who prefers a showerproof coat that doesn't look much like a raincoat, you might consider a double-knit or synthetic-blend all-weather coat that looks like an elegant topcoat but has been chemically treated to be undaunted by either rain or stain. Particularly sporty is the double knit in a robust herringbone pattern. And if you like a *wet look,* investigate the vinyl-coated cotton canvas raincoats.

Casual outerwear styles have, in a few cases, moved over into rainwear. There are safari-style raincoats, for example, with buttoned flap pockets and half belt.

Raincoat lengths go all the way from above the knee right down to the shin-flapping maxi length. The latter is, of course, a very practical rainy-day length, but most men still seem to prefer something shorter.

You should give some thought to the lining of your raincoat. Do you want it to be removable and in that way set the coat up for wear throughout even the frostiest months? A lining of wool or simulated fur can turn any warm-weather raincoat into a year-round garment. Regular raincoat linings of the permanent, non-zip-out variety are usually of a smooth, lustrous material and are often checked, striped or plaid.

If you want your coat to be machine washable, be sure to read the label. If for some reason it doesn't read loud and clear, make a point of asking your salesman. Machine washing versus dry cleaning might be of no particular consequence to you, but then again it might be. Especially if you settle for a white or light shade.

Rubbers

In London, where rain is practically a member of the family, many men show a haughty disdain for rubbers, despite their obvious and total respect for fine shoes. We don't suggest you follow their example. Instead have not one but two pairs of rubbers: one for home, the other for the office. Get the full-bodied kind that really cover the shoe. Today they're so light and supple, they fold up into a plastic envelope. And for near-blizzard weather there are stretch rubber boots that will protect your trouser legs; they're so supple, too, that when not in use they fold up into *their* plastic envelope. (Some men prefer to forget all about rubbers in favor of no-nonsense boots and demiboots.)

Headgear

The plastic-bag-over-the-hat routine has all but disappeared from the rainy-day scene, and good riddance. It was enough to give any man a Caspar Milquetoast aura and furthermore it was never a necessity. Rain does *not* hurt a felt hat, so let it get wet. But if you'd like to have something especially jaunty for rainy-day wear, try a cap or one of the soft cloth hats in a plaid or check or a solid shade.

Umbrellas

Invest in a pair of these, too. The tote kind telescopes down into a zippered plastic tube that can slip into an attaché case or coat pocket. It's eminently practical for keeping in the bottom drawer of your desk, just in case. The other umbrella should be a full-scale model, black and sporting a handsome handle. A blatantly optimistic note for a gray day is the giant multicolored golf umbrella that is now being sold for just plain rainy-day duty.

HATS

What John Fitzgerald Kennedy did for the two-button suit, he did *not* do for the hat. Even in the most severe weather, JFK would appear hatless, snowflakes flecking the famous Kennedy thatch—a many-splendored thing all too rarely seen atop a man of forty-plus, and for that reason alone a point of pride as well as a distinguishing feature for a media-conscious politico. It is hardly surprising that hatlessness was thus encouraged among many of the young who were almost excessively hair-conscious. In any event, the hat is still far from extinct, and in the opinion of *Esquire*'s fashion department, "Hats complete the look and add the proper touch of insouciance."

While brims go from broad to narrow and back to broad again, and crowns go up and down like the Dow-Jones average, one thing is certain: few men can wear every hat style. All of us have our limitations dictated by facial contours and general physique. But before we get down to specifics, here's one rule that applies to all: Before you buy a hat, make certain to take a long, cool look at yourself wearing that hat in a full-length mirror. Chic women never fail to put their chapeaux to this sensible head-to-toe test, but for some reason few men do.

Styles to Suit Your Face

The long, narrow face. Even if you're a six-footer, you can't carry too much hat. By that we mean a full crown, wide band and brim, all of which tends to give you a pinched look. Your best style is a low, tapered crown and a moderate brim. Still, there are exceptions. For example, a tall man with sufficiently square shoulders, may—despite a long, narrow face—look plenty dashing in the very broad-brimmed planter's hat. But once again it's a question of how he's put together. The point we're making is simply this: a long, narrow face dictates a certain basic style of hat, but now and then you may find you can wear another style that is quite different. But first things first: know your style before you start getting adventurous.

The round face. Avoid hats with sharply tapered crowns and narrow brims, and low-crown porkpie hats; it's the old bit about the peanut atop the barrel. Your hat should create the illusion of a longer, narrower face and nothing does that quite like a full crown with medium brim. So no matter how big a comeback the derby may make, avoid it. And while the semiformal homburg may do you in, there is a more full-crowned version that some but not all round faces can wear.

The square face. Yours is a rugged face and you want a hat that will round off the corners. A low-tapered crown with a very narrow brim won't do it, but a full crown with a medium brim will. On the other hand, you may be able to sport a broader brim depending on your height, all of which brings us back to that full-length-mirror test.

The oval face. You have a nicely balanced face and a nicely balanced hat is what it asks for. So opt for the medium-height, tapered-crown style with a moderate brim. Eschew the full crown with wide brim. The semiformal homburg should look great on you. Ditto most of the sporty, shapelier models.

Classic Hat Styles

The following are classic hat styles, from which any number of variations derive:

Snap brim. This is the hat of the twentieth century. It is made of felt, and you can wear it more than any other hat you own. You can shape it any way you want (the shape can be steamed in, after which it remains there permanently until you steam it out and steam another shape in), but the most common is the "pinched crown." This has a dent going lengthwise down the top, and two pinches in the sides in front. Depending on the shape of your head, the center crease might be varied slightly into a triangular shape, but all in all it's the same style. The snap brim is turned down across the front, and its edges can either be turned back (a sort of welt seam with no stitching) or bound with a ribbed silk fabric. The band is most often made of grosgrain, although suede, velvet, fur and fake fur bands have gained in popularity during the era of the wide-brimmed style. These so-called Gangster Hat or Boutique Brim snap brims complement wider suit lapels and wider neckties via brims often measuring about 3½ inches (versus a medium brim of about 1¾ inches), and this added width invariably means a higher crown for the sake of balance.

Homburg. A formal hat, with a rolled brim at the sides and a forward and aft dip, the homburg has a tapered crown. The edges of the brim are curled slightly. This modern equivalent of the bowler is now more or less relegated to being worn with formal evening and formal day clothes.

Shaped hat. This style has a side roll that is more exaggerated than that in the homburg; a tapered crown with deep roll of the brim at the sides and a forward dip. Depending on the felt— smooth or rough—it is acceptable for business, sports and casual wear.

Fur hat. Like the fur coat, the fur hat can be practically duplicated (for a fraction of the cost) by the furlike hat of a synthetic fiber or blend of fibers. The cossack style dominates and for a good reason: it seems to have the uncanny knack of looking good on every shape face.

Cloth hat: A sportswear classic usually made of wool, in plaid, check or a diagonal weave. Although it had been around for years, it didn't really gain widespread popularity until it was worn by Professor 'enry 'iggins (Rex Harrison) in *My Fair Lady.*

Suede hat. This hat has a tapered crown with a narrow brim in brushed-surface leather or another material. Primarily a sports hat, it combines especially well with tweed jackets, suits and topcoats.

Tyrolean hat: Adapted closely from the yodeler's hat, it's made of smooth- or rough-surface felt or a lustrous velour. The band is composed of three or four cords instead of ribbon, and there is a brush instead of a bow. A very jaunty model that gained world-wide fame in the thirties when it was popularized by the trend-setting Prince of Wales.

HATS

Snap-brim   Pinched-crown   Low-crown snap-brim

Homburg   Shaped hat   Cloth

Suede   Tyrolean   Porkpie

Porkpie hat. A snap brim with tapered crown, flattened top (no center crease) and relatively narrow ribbon, it came here via England and was immensely popular for both business and sportswear. Today it is seen mostly in a soft cloth golf hat.

Hidden-visor cap. A cloth cap, the top of which snaps onto the visor, concealing it. Once very much in evidence on golf courses and on the grounds of English manors. Always popular with knicker suits. Wool caps are worn in cold weather, and for the warmer seasons there are cotton models.

Boater or sennit

Planter's

Coconut palm

Milan

Center-crease

Optimo

Hidden-visor cap

Beret

Cossack-style

Beret. Until the Special Forces of the American Army started wearing green berets, this hat was primarily thought of as French, which after all it is. The Americanization of the beret has, however, not altered its personality one iota. It is still a very sporty item and worn accordingly.

Milan hat. With a "telescope" crown, this model is of fine-stitched braid material and may be trimmed with a pleated pugree in patterned or solid-color fabric.

Boater or sennit. A flat-top straw with stiff top, sides and brim; no snap brim, no center crease, no pinch. Usually trimmed with a striped ribbon band, it's a smart-looking echo of the twenties that has been taken up by some of the younger men, who wear it with both blazers and business suits.

Center-crease summer hat. This hat may be in Panama, Milan, coconut or other material. It's trimmed with a striped ribbon band, and is most popular today for resort wear with sport shirts and slacks.

Optimo-shape Panama. Has a tropical air about it. Although it has been made in coconut palm or raffia as well as the light Panama straw, when it made its comeback along with the all-white summer suit in the late sixties, it was seen most often in Panama.

Planter's hat. A very broad-brimmed hat originally worn in the tropics by owners and workers on plantations. Though it is essentially a resort or beach hat, some men have taken to wearing variations of it in town.

Coconut palm. This hat is made of a coarse braid and trimmed with a pugree. The outstanding feature of this material is its dark shade.

Just as with shoes, there are styles here that are rarely seen today. The fashion impact of such hats has been considerable, however, and variations of these styles (and very often the original itself) will continue to have influence.

HOW TO TAKE CARE OF YOUR HATS

There is only one way to put on a hat without bending the brim out of shape: Hold the brim in the front and back with both hands and place the hat on your head at a slight angle to the left or to the right.

Felt hats should be brushed regularly with a soft-bristled brush. Always brush with the nap of the surface.

Rain doesn't harm felt. If you get caught in the rain, simply put your hat on a shelf to dry, with the sweatband turned out. Brush it when it has dried completely.

CHAPTER SEVEN

Nightwear and Underwear

A PEACOCK doesn't stop showing his plumage simply because the lights are doused and it's time to retire. Not today when sleepwear boasts so much style and offers a man such variety.

"Meant-to-be-seen fashions that would just as soon leisure around as snooze" is the way one New York department store put it in a recent ad, turning thumbs down on what the copywriter called "safe, classic pajamas." And reflecting this attitude are many contemporary pajamas that have such a well-tailored sporty look about them that if a man wearing one of this genre happened to be vacationing at a summer resort, he could practically tumble out of bed and go to the patio for breakfast looking perfectly proper.

PAJAMAS

Not that the classic pajama has faded from the scene. Far from it. Manufacturers are still turning them out in exciting colors and patterns, and in a fabric range extending from such staples as broadcloth and oxford, through manmade fibers such as acetate rayon and all-polyester, to the latest body-conforming knits. The classic pj is just that—a pajama with no pretense of being anything else. And among the most durable classics are the two following best sellers:

Coat style. The top is styled like a sports jacket with a button-front closure, long sleeves and a modified collar. With it go long trousers with either an elastic waistband and snap fastener or a cord.

Collarless coat. The upper in this style resembles a cardigan. It has a plain edge, a single chest pocket or a chest pocket with two lower pockets. There may be long trousers as described above or short ones for midsummer wear.

Many of the latest avant-garde pajamas are spin-offs from these two classics but the relationship appears to be so remote that most manufacturers and retailers refer to them as *Loungewear* rather than pajamas. And in fact they often more closely resemble a casual suit than a pajama.

Dominant are those with a military or active-sportswear look: the "Ike" combat-type jacket teamed up with trousers styled like slacks; the safari or bush jacket top replete with deep pockets and epaulets, worn with slacklike trousers. Either or both models might be made of a sturdy stretch denim. The Ike outfit is especially becoming to a short man, since the jacket is waist length and therefore gives the illusion of longer legs. The safari model, on the other hand, is catnip for the tall, thin man since the pockets and epaulets create a horizontal effect and the longer jacket seems to subtract inches from the length of the legs.

Naturally, the knits with their built-in guarantee of comfort are rampant in sleepwear. A knit jump suit pajama certainly earns the tag of *Leisurewear*, but only a perfect or near-perfect physical specimen should take on the jump suit pj with tank top which, patterned after the tank swimsuit, is sleeveless, with skinny shoulder straps and a deep U neckline front and back. And the same note of caution applies to some of the summer-weight sleep shorts in "air-conditioned" cloths—the ones so short they've been referred to as hot pants.

Much easier to wear well are the updated versions of the old-time nightshirt. In knee or just-above-the-knee length, they're available in everything from fireman red flannel to synthetic fabrics emblazoned with barber pole stripes. Some men prefer theirs with long sleeves, and others want half sleeves. Some want a nightshirt with an all-around belt or side tie, while the purist opts for the classic, straight-hanging lines. (And there are some men who insist on a button front so they can slip their nightshirt on like a coat, instead of pulling it over the head.) In some places it's called a sleep coat, and somewhere else (provided it has a belt or side tie) it may be known as a shave coat. But you'll have no trouble recognizing it for what it is, a freewheeling translation of Gramp's one-piece night garment.

As you can readily see, there's something for everyone. And traditionalist though you may be, we suggest you express your individuality via a few of the so-called loungewear models, too. A strong point in their favor is that most of them are styled to encourage mixing the top of this one with the bottom of that one so that before you know it you've got yourself a highly imaginative sleepwear wardrobe of contrasting fabrics and patterns.

ROBES AND SLIPPERS

Robes, too, come in a variety that's truly eye-popping—all the way from the one-size-fits-all kimono of lightweight cotton to the shawl-collared, ankle-length robe of silk twill. No wonder today's man wears a robe around the house to lounge, where once he regarded a robe as just something handy for keeping warm. In fact, there are even some notch-collar robe models that, replete with wide lapels, tie belt and pleated patch pockets, reproduce the sporty look of casual suits or topcoats.

It's up to you to pick what suits your personality. Ideal, we think, for spring-summer wear would be one of the kimono- or toga-style robes in perhaps a neat foulard print or jacquard pattern or a vivid solid color; and for fall-winter wear, a wool with the fitted shoulders and buttoned pleated pockets of a safari jacket; or a longer, dressier robe in a frankly lush fabric such as lightweight silk or supple velour—pure elegance right down to the fringed sash.

With pajamas and robes making such a splash these days, only a dullard would think of stuffing his bare feet into a pair of scuffed old felt slippers without experiencing a twinge of conscience. After all, slippers are as important a feature of the new sleepwear/loungewear look as pajamas and robes, and just as every suit of clothes won't take the same style of shoe, the look of the pj-robe combination dictates the style of slipper. The moccasin type, for example, is appropriate with the short-legged pajama worn with kimono- or toga-style robe, but the longer, dressier robe asks for something more sophisticated, like a hand-turned slipper or mule of kidskin or suede leather. And should you put on a silk or velour robe with fringed sash, we suggest you settle for nothing less than a velvet or patent leather slip-on with instep bow—almost grand enough to double as an evening pump.

UNDERWEAR

Shapelier clothes beget shapelier underwear. So contemporary underwear fits more like a second skin—not too tight to squeeze, not too loose to wrinkle and sag. And while "basic white" continues to be the dominant look, color has been making inroads, along with some mighty eye-arresting patterns.

"Start a fashion revolution from within," urged a 1971 department store ad for underwear in *The New York Times*, featuring bikini and mini-bikini briefs in black, gold, red and royal blue. Yet T-shirts and boxer shorts are still very much with us.

Here's how the current crop of underwear stacks up:

Undershirts

T-shirt. The classic model featuring short sleeves, crew neck and straight bottom is still the leader. But there are interesting variations: a V neckline to wear under open-collar shirts; a deep scoop neckline for sport shirts; and a raglan-sleeve model with a mock turtleneck that's made to order for the cold weather. A *tapered* T-shirt has these distinctions: slightly shorter, slimmer sleeves than the classic model, and a minimum 4-inch taper.

Athletic shirt. Less popular than the T-shirt but still claiming its devotees is this sleeveless shirt, with thin bands of fabric extending over the shoulders from a wide U-shaped front and back. Almost always in a white ribbed knitted cotton, the athletic shirt every now and then shows up in a solid color with contrasting trim.

Undershorts

Boxers. Loose-fitting shorts resembling a prizefighter's trunks, with an unfastened fly front and a waistband that's either snap-fastened or crimped elastic sans any closure. An updated version,

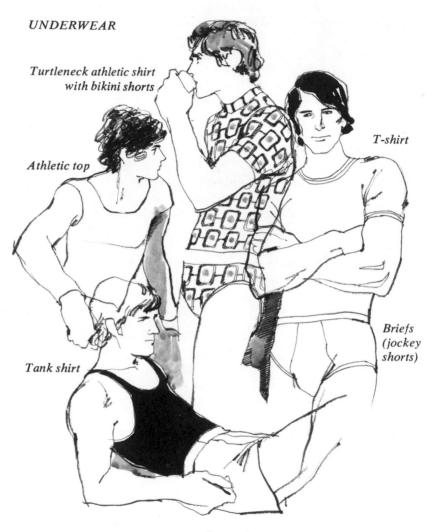

UNDERWEAR

**Turtleneck athletic shirt
with bikini shorts**

Athletic top

T-shirt

Tank shirt

**Briefs
(jockey
shorts)**

Boxer shorts

often referred to as boxer briefs, has less fabric, a lower rise, shorter leg and, occasionally, side vents. Still seen mostly in solid colors, boxers also are available in patterns.

Briefs. A knitted short with pouch front, no legs and an elasticized waistband. Costlier styles are made from a number of separate panels, while less expensive models have fewer. A variation is the *support* or *slimming brief*, featuring a higher waistband that can compress a waistline as much as 2 inches.

Bikini. The brief-brief modeled after the bikini swimwear first worn on the French Riviera. To say that it requires a minimum of fabric (generally a synthetic like acrylic knit or nylon tricot) is an understatement, but then there's the mini-bikini brief that's scarcely more than an athletic supporter with side slits.

One-Piece Underwear

There are two variations on this theme. One is a waist-to-toe solid-color knit undergarment with ribbed dress socks, an offshoot of women's pantyhose. Touted as providing warmth without bulky weight, one size stretches to fit all. One drawback: the single size may contain too much fabric around the waist area for smaller people.

The other variation is a body suit, usually of woven nylon, with short sleeves, no legs and, sometimes, a button front and long fashion collar allowing it to double as a form-fitting sport shirt. Particularly noteworthy is a knit body shirt that boasts a snap crotch. Result: a wrinkle-proof torso shirt from the waist up— and from the waist down, a pair of comfortable shorts.

The body shirt is mostly available in solid colors (would you believe pink and soft blue?), although it can also be had in contrasting color combinations and any number of patterns.

Cotton, nylon and polyester-cotton blends are the leading underwear fabrics. Here's how they're rated:

Cotton. Easy to wash and absorbent, but can lose its shape and shrink, unless treated.

Nylon. It won't shrink, or lose its shape while being worn, but it isn't absorbent and clings to the body.

Polyester-cotton blends. Hold shape better and are more durable than cotton; more absorbent than nylon but less so than cotton. These blends can shrink somewhat, however, depending on their cotton content.

HOW TO TAKE CARE OF UNDERWEAR

Wash (read manufacturer's instructions about bleach) and either tumble or hand dry. For cotton and blends, use hot water; for nylon, warm water. Nylon should also be dried on the warm, never the hot, drying setting. Cottons retain shape better if machine dried; nylons last longer when hand washed and hang dried.

Casual Outerwear

THESE rugged and sporty coats and jackets are a true slice of Americana, for no man enjoys them so much or wears them so well as the American. His unadulterated passion for casual outerwear has ignited similar enthusiasm among younger Europeans, and a tour through Paris, Copenhagen and some of the more fashion-conscious capitals finds copies of this typically American apparel giving the landscape an incongruously Yankee flavor.

Casual outerwear really came into its own during the post-World War II period, and then in the wake of the fashion revolution fairly exploded with new styles and fabrics. Today in many of the larger American cities there has been an increasing acceptance of this garb not only for the odd weekend hours in suburbia, but for the conventional weekday hours of nine to five in town, with the result that denim and leather—once generally considered exclusively country sportswear—have become almost citified.

The following is a rundown of the most prevalent casual outerwear styles from which scores of variations are constantly spinning off:

Battle Jacket

Also known as the mess or Ike jacket in recognition of the fact that it at least began its civilian fashion life as a copy of the waist-length jacket generally associated with General Dwight D. Eisenhower. Today's versions are often somewhat longer and sometimes fleece lined, but the general characteristics, whether the jacket is in leather, denim, suede or corduroy, are fairly constant: snap closures down the front; a lie-down, shirtlike collar; a straight bottom; and button or snap shirt-style cuffs.

This is especially flattering to the short man since it tends to give the wearer a leggy look, and for that reason it's far from flattering for the tall, thin man.

Pea Coat

A direct steal from the pea coat of the U.S. Navy; in fact, many of them worn by the under-25 crowd were picked up at Army-Navy surplus stores. Always the regulation eight-button, double-breasted model, though the fabric may vary; preferred, however, is navy blue melton cloth.

Safari Jacket

Also known as a bush jacket, it's so versatile that it has turned up as the top half of casual suits or pajamas; with matching shorts it's often seen as part of a two-piece beach ensemble. As a result, the single-breasted safari jacket derived from the jacket worn by the big-game hunter fits into several apparel categories besides casual outerwear. Be that as it may, the styling features of the safari jacket, with or without epaulets, remain constant: four flapped patch pockets in front; button closures; and an all-around belt. Its robust styling and over-the-seat length make it particularly attractive for the tall, thin man.

Mackinaw

A perennial favorite and still another coat style especially becoming to the tall, thin man. Features a broad shawl collar, big pockets, belt and over-the-seat length. Originally in bold, colorful country plaids, the mackinaw today comes in a variety of fabrics, patterns and colors.

Parka

Back in '62, *Esquire* noted "the progress of the parka" not only on the nation's ski slopes, where it first appeared, but on campuses as well. Soon after, it was credited with inspiring a new 32-inch casual coat and influencing the styling of reversible coats. Today's parka is a casual outerwear classic in nylon or pile, with a zipper front, hood and a spread or stand-up military collar.

Trench Coat

Still another example of the tremendous influence the military has on men's apparel. After starting out in life as an all-weather cotton gabardine coat providing foul-weather protection for World War I doughboys fighting in the trenches, it carried over into civilian life and became a rainwear classic. Most recently, the mid-calf-length trench coat, in leather, pigskin suede or pile-lined denim, has moved over into casual outerwear, where it's often labeled a *storm coat*. Styling features include: epaulets; cuff flaps; front and/or back yoke; scalloped flaps on large patch pockets.

Wrap Coat

This is a buttonless double-breasted coat with a self-belt, and in, say, a fleecy wool and a dressy knee or below-the-knee length it can qualify as a striking topcoat. In a gutsier fabric and fingertip length it is casual outerwear with an uncommon amount of swagger.

Duffel Coat

A knee-length coat usually in a heavy tan or navy melton cloth, it features a bucket hood; cylindrical or horn-shaped buttons that fasten through a loop of rope instead of a buttonhole; large flapped patch pockets; and often body-tracing sides. It makes an excellent car coat.

AN OUTERWEAR VOCABULARY

Bal collar. A short, stand-up collar resembling a shirt collar; it can be worn up or folded over.

Bucket hood. As seen on the duffel coat, it hangs in back like a pouch. Some, however, are attached to the coat via buttons or a zipper and can be detached.

Concealed hood. As the name implies, it is concealed within the collar of the coat or jacket (the parka has a concealed hood, for example) and is held in place by buttons or a zipper.

Convertible collar. Usually seen on parkas, it looks like a spread collar and can be zipped all the way up to what would be the collar tips, closing it into a pseudo turtleneck.

Raglan sleeve. Seams extend from the armhole to the neck in front and back of the coat, converging at the collar line.

Saddle shoulder. A version of the raglan sleeve, but instead of converging at the collar, the seams extend to it, remaining parallel.

Set-in sleeve. The same sleeve as in suit jackets; a seam is visible where the sleeve is joined to the coat's body, while another is centered along the shoulder from the collar line to the sleeve.

Split shawl collar. Especially dashing, it extends in an uninterrupted line completely around the neck and down to the coat's top button, but then becomes separated into an upper and lower portion at the collarbone; the upper portion can usually remain up around the back of the head as protection against inclement weather. This collar is usually the same color and fabric as the rest of the coat, but it is sometimes covered with pile or fur.

Split shoulder. A hybrid—a combination of the raglan and the set-in sleeve.

Spread collar. Very much like a spread collar on a sport shirt, it spreads out and lies down flat.

HOW TO TAKE CARE OF CASUAL OUTERWEAR

Garments of weather-proofed fabrics generally need reprocessing after a few cleanings.

In the case of a stain on a suede jacket, rub it with a plastic eraser, sandpaper or an emery board.

Smooth-finish leathers can be washed with a sponge and a light solution of liquid detergent, finishing off with clean water.

Leather may be pressed by placing a sheet of brown paper over it and using a warm (not hot) iron.

CHAPTER NINE

Sportswear

This particular category of apparel was once upon a time restricted to weekend or country wear, and only on a Saturday would a businessman dare to drop by his office garbed in sports jacket and slacks. Today, of course, the distinctions between what is sportswear and what is businesswear have blurred, and although the suit is still—in most offices—the appropriate thing to wear to business, a more relaxed, easy-to-be-in outfit is gaining acceptance as a substitute. In certain business areas (such as the creative department of an ad agency, the editorial and art departments of a magazine) the sports jacket and slacks are the rule rather than the exception.

FOR THE SPECTATOR

So let's zero in on the blazer, which some fashion pundits have dubbed the "everything coat."

The Blazer

Just as no one can sensibly discuss rainwear without paying special attention to the trench coat, no one can discuss sportswear without paying special attention to the jacket that was first worn aboard H.M.S. *Blazer* back in the 1860s. In this century the blazer jacket came into its own as sportswear in the thirties when, as one fashion reporter covering the Palm Beach scene noted, that fashionable resort was "ablaze with flannel blazers." But not until the sixties, with the universal acceptance of informal dress, did the blazer jacket really move into the city and settle down. Today a solid-

BLAZERS

color or patterned blazer, single- or double-breasted, worn with a pair of slacks, solid-color or patterned, comprise a fashionable outfit for both town (with shirt and tie) and country (with open-necked shirt and ascot scarf).

But that's only skimming the surface. The blazer of the seventies may also be the jacket of a blazer suit, so today's blazer is really a many-splendored thing and when backed up with the right variety of shirts, slacks and ties it's almost unbelievably versatile. Take, for example, the solid-color denim blazer that comes piped in a contrasting color—say, a hunter green blazer with yellow piping along the lapels, continuing on down the front of the jacket and just beginning to curve around the skirt before it stops cold. Feed a blazer like that a dress shirt—perhaps a yellow or bone-color solid or one making capital of those colors in a check or plaid—add a beige silk tie and a pair of gray double-knit slacks, and you've got yourself a great in-town outfit.

Now feed this same denim blazer a sport shirt and a pair of tartan plaid or gingham check jeans, and nobody but nobody will color a country landscape quite like you.

A satin blazer? Yes, a *satin* blazer. In ruby red or deep purple or bottle green. Not for every man, it's true, but if you can carry it off (meaning financially as well as poisewise, since a satin blazer that's really well tailored will carry a price tag of $150-plus) this is a remarkably handsome jacket. Satin, of course, demands the more formal double-breasted styling and coupled with satin slacks of a contrasting color adds up to a smashing suit for the cocktail hour. Accessories are rather tricky. For instance, you certainly wouldn't wear an oxford shirt with satin blazer and satin slacks. Only a solid-color silk shirt will do. Then tie on a richly patterned silk tie (the only pattern you're wearing), and that's that. Not so much as a pocket handkerchief is necessary.

How do you convert a satin blazer into a sporty outfit? Simple. Just peel off your silk shirt and tie and put on a long-sleeved sport shirt of a not-too-bold print. Just as an oxford dress shirt would be all wrong with a satin blazer, so would a rough-textured sport shirt; the fabric must have sheen, and one that does and that we heartily recommend is a polished cotton.

The *velvet* blazer in a shade of emerald green, bottle green, ruby red, burgundy red, navy blue or deep chocolate is a positive stunner. More often than not, the coat is half of a blazer suit and as such is a workhorse. It's a fantastic suit to wear to a cocktail party, and if you work in a truly liberated atmosphere it's also a casually elegant business suit. Exchange the velvet trousers for slacks—perhaps a giant houndstooth or tartan pattern—and your dress shirt and tie for a white turtleneck pullover, and you're togged out for a country picnic of the type where the wicker basket holds pumpernickel, pungent cheeses, chilled grapes and plenty of chilled *vino*.

The Blazer Suit/The Sport Suit/The Country Suit

Confusing, isn't it? Where does one leave off and the other begin? Well, the blazer suit and the sport suit are actually one and the same. Some manufacturers advertise their blazer suits as sport suits, while others do just the opposite. We explored the blazer suit in depth in our Suits chapter and briefly it is this: a city suit in a blazer fabric, whose jacket is sporty-looking enough to double as a sports jacket. (See why some manufacturers choose to call it a "sport suit"?) The jacket's trim—which is often its extraordinary buttons—and cut qualify the suit to be called a blazer suit. As a result, today we have blazer suits in everything from plush velvet to sturdy denim, their jackets all going solo as sports jackets by merely substituting a turtleneck pullover or sport shirt for shirt and tie.

The country suit, on the other hand, is a name tag given to a suit that because of its fabric and/or pattern was once upon a time considered proper only for country or suburban wear. A corduroy or denim suit, for instance. Or a bold windowpane plaid. Times have changed and the term *country suit* is frankly obsolete today, although it hangs on simply because it worked its way into our fashion vocabulary long ago. Suffice it to say that today a city suit . . . is a country suit . . . is a city suit. The windowpane plaid once considered too sporty for business is now thoroughly at home in the boardroom, and its suit jacket doubles as a sports jacket on weekends. Ditto the sturdy denim, corduroy and camel's hair suits, all once considered strictly country suits. On the other hand, a citified suit like a herringbone knit or a gabardine worn with pullover or sport shirt can automatically become a country suit.

So you see, the fashion movement works both ways and, as a result, today there are innumerable suits that, with an artful switch of accessories, perform handsomely in both town and country.

The Casual Suit

The casual suit is the ultimate in comfort. Or, as we put it back in our Suits chapter, "its purpose in life is to make the wearer look and feel great when he's not doing anything in particular." Under the circumstances is it any wonder the casual suit has become a fashion phenomenon, and that today it's as snappy for Sunday brunch-running as it is when you're "not doing anything in particular"?

So doesn't it stand to reason that you should own at least one casual suit? And don't assume that it has to be a knit simply because so many are. The safari suit is perhaps the most popular of all casual suits for the good reason that it's so flattering to most men, and it comes in denim, cotton canvas, velvet, gabardine, linen, wool, chamois, corduroy, sailcloth, calf suede—and that's only a partial list.

Ever since Richard Nixon's visit to China, the amply pocketed, easy-wearing Mao jacket has infiltrated into the ranks of the casual suit, shouldering its way alongside such classics as the Eisenhower jacket and the bush jacket. And why not? What with jeans having started out as the work pants of the hard-working cowpoke, and many of today's jump suits clearly showing their descent from the work clothes of the mechanic or "grease monkey," garb straight from the People's Republic of China fits right in with young America's penchant for dandified work clothes.

Shop around and find the casual suit that suits your physique and personality type. If you're slender and outgoing, you might slip into a tank-topped jump suit, wrap a sash belt around your middle and look the way an F. Scott Fitzgerald hero would had he the chance to start all over again today. But if you're not so slender and have a personality that feels more at ease in something less flashy, investigate a safari suit, a tunic-style suit or a jean suit.

One of the nicest things about owning a casual suit is that most of them, though not all, can lead a double life. A one-piece jump suit, for obvious reasons, can't be worn with the top or bottom half of something else. But the jacket of a safari suit can look a winner worn with anything from a pair of super-soft suede slacks to a pair of jean-styled stretch denim shorts. Wear a tweed tunic with a pair of velvet slacks, and you've got yourself one mighty handsome cocktail time outfit. (Mixing fabrics in your sportswear wardrobe is as rewarding a fashion pastime as mixing patterns in your business wardrobe.) And couple a Mao jacket with a pair of blue jeans, and this marriage of the inscrutable East with the fathomable West produces an outfit that gives you the best of both worlds.

In short, you owe it to your sportswear wardrobe to give it a casual suit or two or three.

The Sports Jacket

What with all the mixing of suit jackets with slacks, you might think that the sports jacket has lost ground. Does it still have a bona fide place in your wardrobe? You bet it does. All the competition for your attention has inspired designers to outdo themselves, to create sports jackets that can't be ignored by any fashion-conscious man.

Plaid sports jackets are bigger, brighter, more aggressive-looking than ever. A red and green tartan, for instance, looks sensational with a pair of fireman red double-knit slacks. Cotton madras is more popular than ever, and if green's your color, latch on to a cotton madras sports jacket in several shades of green and couple it with a pair of bright yellow slacks. Crisp, crinkly seersucker has made a giant comeback with a new bolder look. Today's seersucker, for example, might feature brisk stripes of alternating hot pink and ice blue. With a jacket like that, pull on a pair of pale blue slacks and the combination will suggest you have a yacht parked at the nearest marina.

Solid colors are still headline-makers—particularly if the color is *red*. With your red sports jacket wear a pair of pale pink slacks, or a pair with tablecloth checks in red and white or red and blue.

Double-knit jackets are seen in everything from geometric patterns to rainbow stripes. With these bold-look jackets, all-white slacks look particularly handsome.

White is a perennial in summer sports jackets. White linen, for instance, looks especially outstanding when worn with jean-styled slacks made of madras patches. Or you might choose a white sports jacket that's splattered with a design—anything from fleurs-de-lis to multicolored cotton patches—and add a pair of white or cream-color slacks for a look of pure elegance.

So if you have the dough, you'll earn dividends by investing some of it in at least two sports jackets for spring-summer and two for fall-winter.

The Sport Shirt

You should have a wardrobe of sport shirts, both short-sleeved and long-sleeved. Open mesh shirts are ideal for hot-weather wear since they allow the air to circulate where it's needed most, and for the cooler days and nights there is the classic sweater shirt with ribbed cuffs and bottom, updated with a longer point collar. A summer cocktail outfit for suburbia or country might well include a tapered, long-sleeved, solid-color or patterned sport shirt, silk ascot, slacks, and white slip-ons, saddle shoes, or solid-color canvas espadrilles. And if the weather threatens to turn cool, add a sports jacket or blazer.

Pantology

The classic blue jeans are year-round sportswear, and denim-patch jeans (great squares of contrasting plain colors or patterns) are a dressier version. Take jeans, add a wool pullover, boots or demiboots—and it all adds up to a great know-no-age sportswear outfit.

Cutoffs—homemade or store-bought, with the ragged-edge scissored look or neat 2-inch cuff—have nudged Bermuda walk shorts out of first place so far as the younger men are concerned. You can create your own thigh-length cutoffs by taking a pair of jeans or slacks and having at them with your scissors, or you can get them ready-made in practically any jeans store and have the choice of ragged edge or neat cuffs. Either way, these short shorts are where it's at at present and if you're young enough and slim enough, get 'em and wear 'em. They look fine with any number of different tops: a safari or Eisenhower jacket . . . a turtleneck pullover . . . a sport shirt . . . or, if the time and place are right, no top at all. (Knee-length cutoffs with scissored edges are okay, too, if the shorter version is too short for you.)

Meanwhile, although the longer Bermuda walk shorts have dipped in popularity, knickers have come back on a wave of nostalgia for the twenties and thirties. Some of the younger men tuck them into boots and top them with turtleneck pullovers and sometimes a cap. All of which makes for a dandy cycling outfit.

Sweaters

Sweaters are absolutely essential to your sportswear wardrobe. The white V-neck tennis sweater with navy and red border stripes is a summertime classic, even miles away from a tennis court. The sweater vest is an ideal accessory for the cooler-weather sports jacket. And patterned sleeveless pullovers and cardigans look splendid worn over double-knit sport shirts of matching or contrasting patterns.

And since fashion continues to churn up a revolution in sweaters, it's important that you know some of the basic truths about them. We suggest, therefore, that you check with the Sweater Guide you'll find at the end of this chapter.

As you can see, the term *sportswear* has been elasticized until today it stretches in all directions. Now that women can wear pants to the best places and even the staid Metropolitan Opera probably wouldn't turn away a ticket holder togged out in a safari suit, sportswear has taken on a whole new complexion. In the past, many a fashion classic first saw the light of day in sportswear and then proceeded to work its way into a man's nine-to-five wardrobe. But today, with the emphasis on comfort and more informal dress, the list of apparel that can be classified as strictly sportswear is almost certain to shrink. More and more, what you wear and when and where you wear it will be a question of your own good taste, and that of course is what this book is all about.

SWEATER GUIDE

Collars

Bib. An insert of contrasting or self fabric set into a V-neck.

Continental. Similar to a sport shirt collar in appearance, with a wide spread.

Convertible. This is a spread collar with a zipper running to the end. It can be worn either as a turtleneck (rolled over), or as a continental collar (spread).

Johnny. Usually a small roll collar.

Military. A stand-up collar, about 1 inch high with a split in front.

Notched. Two-piece construction with a V-shaped wedge at the point where the lapel meets the collar.

Shawl. Similar to the clothing model that eliminates the lapel. The curved collar continues its line without a break to the top button.

Necklines

Boat neck. Cut straight across the shoulder, extending almost to the shoulder points. Has a slit or horizontal line, and may have ribbing in the back.

Crew neck. Classic round- or ring-shaped neckline. Can be squared, too.

High V neck. This one drops 5 to 5½ inches.

Regular V neck. Tapers to a point about 8½ inches from the top of the V.

Turtleneck. It forms a cuff at the neckline and folds over about

SWEATER (necklines)

Mock turtle

Round neck

Turtleneck

Crew neck

Cardigan

V-neck plus turtleneck

2 to 3 inches. The so-called mock turtleneck does not have the folded-over cuff, although it's as high as the regular turtleneck.

Sleeves

Bell. The taper is almost completely eliminated in a bell sleeve— i.e., it has equal width throughout to the cuff—to give a full effect in the forearm. Cuff is sewn and looped on.

Dolman (or batwing). The front of the sleeve and the body is one piece of fabric; same with the back of the sleeve and body. Both are joined at top and bottom edges of the sleeves.

Modified bell. A straight sleeve that does taper somewhat.

Tapered. Most sweaters have sleeves that taper to the wrist or cuff. This tapering is machine-made on full-fashion garments; done by hand on cut-and-sewns. (*Full-fashion* means that the garment was knit to shape on the machine.)

Shoulders

Raglan. The sleeves extend into the shoulder, ending at the neck in a point.

Saddle. At the armhole this shoulder is similar to the raglan, and it likewise ends at the neckline. However, the shoulder "cap" runs in a parallel line to the neckline, about 3 to 5 inches in width.

Set-in. This is the standard shirt construction applied to sweaters. The sleeve is joined to the body along a vertical seam that circles the top of the arm or armhole.

Split. A combination shoulder that's usually a set-in in the front (vertical armhole seaming) and raglan (extended to the neckline) in the rear portion.

HOW TO TAKE CARE OF YOUR SWEATERS

Today most wool sweaters are machine washable. In fact, when the hangtag specifies *Washable*, it invariably means *machine washable* —that's how commonplace machine washable wool sweaters (and shirts) have become. Still, you should read the manufacturer's washing recommendations carefully before you toss your sweater into the machine. And yes, you may still find that some multicolored wool sweaters are recommended for dry cleaning only, chiefly because the manufacturers fear the colors might run. (Since some men have a little difficulty differentiating between what is meant by a soap and what is meant by a detergent, here are the bare facts: when a hangtag says *soap* it means flakes or bar; *detergent* means a liquid or a powder.)

Washable wool. First turn the sweater inside out; this protects the surface and helps the sweater look new longer; it also keeps any pockets from catching on the inner workings of the washing machine. Set machine at the Gentle or Normal cycle and set water temperature at Warm, which is about 100 degrees F. Wash with any mild soap or detergent. *Do not overwash.* (Check hangtag. Some wool sweaters can go full Normal cycle, which is about fourteen minutes, but others should wash no more than three to five minutes.) Rinse on complete Normal cycle. Next machine (tumble) dry on Normal setting about ten to fifteen minutes. In other words, remove sweater from the dryer while it still contains some moisture. Hang on plastic hanger to dry completely. Blocking is unnecessary.

If for any reason you prefer to *hand wash* your wool sweater, here's what you do:

Turn sweater inside out. Put it in room-temperature water (up to 100 degrees F. versus the usual 65–70 degrees F. of most tap water). Use any normal laundry detergent and let sweater soak for a few minutes, using your hand to move the garment about gently in the water, making sure the water circulates through the fibers. Rinse in clear water at room temperature, again moving the sweater about gently in the water. Squeeze (do not wring) dry. Lay sweater out flat on a towel to lose some moisture before hanging on plastic hanger to dry completely. (If sweater is an exceptionally heavy one and it's hung while still very damp, the "drag" of the moisture can distort shape.) Blocking is unnecessary.

ACTIVE SPORTSWEAR

Long before the fashion revolution, the golfer and skier were displaying their plumage via togs that were ablaze with color. Since the revolution, however, even tennis (often referred to as "the most genteel of sports") has taken on some color. The 1968 Davis Cup team of the U.S. Lawn Tennis Association, for instance, sported yellows and blues, relegating white to their sneakers. In the traditionally all-white world of tennis this was tantamount to a bride wearing a red wedding veil.

But despite the splash of color, rules of attire still count for something in most sports. The rigors of the sport and the season(s) during which it's pursued automatically impose certain restrictions on what the sportsman can wear. (It's unlikely, for example, you'll ever see seersucker in a duck blind.) And furthermore, good sportsmanship dictates that a man dress in a manner that dignifies his sport.

Now let's take up each sport in its turn and suggest how you can dress in a manner that's both functional and fashionable.

Skiing

Except in those far northern countries where skis are a means of practical locomotion as well as sport, skiing has traditionally started out as the rich man's sport before moving down the social scale to the middle classes. Consequently, ski clothes have always had plenty of color and style along with functionalism.

Sensible skiers all dress by an unofficial "layer principle" designed to keep them warm in the teeth of icy winds. All of which takes some skillful shopping since the skier must remain mobile despite the layers of clothing if he's going to be able to twist and turn on the slopes.

The knitted wool cap, with or without tassel, looks very St. Moritz; the knitted wool headband is brief and practical; but nothing is more practical and *today* than the visored ski helmet in a bright yellow-tangerine color—a spin-off from our trip to the moon.

Good choices: the nylon wind jacket and matching pants; nylon parka with front or side zipper, over a wool turtleneck pullover, and matching nylon pants. More offbeat is the cotton denim jacket and pants with a jeans look; the one-piece stretch nylon jump suit with allover stitch pleating, zipper chest pockets and cinch belt.

Wear net underwear for insulation, and for added warmth you might consider one of the snap-front nylon vests that sport fleece on the reverse side.

It's fur-lined gloves, fur or quilted mittens, leather-palmed fabric knits, or quilted leather gloves for your hands, and two pairs of socks—heavy ribbed woolens plus thin cottons—under your ski boots.

Goggles or sunglasses are absolutely essential for reducing the glare of sun or snow.

Tennis

Like skiing, tennis started out as a rich man's sport. After all, only a gentleman of some means could afford the laundry bill for a sport that demanded all-white togs. The sudden dip into color of the last few years is all the more remarkable when you consider that the tennis establishment has always been stiff-necked about its traditions. This is not to suggest that color is running wild on the courts just yet. But that it has dared to show up at all is a matter of some consequence.

Every now and then, if the sun is particularly bright, a man will slap on a sun visor, but it's rare. Hatlessness is the order of this sport.

A knitted cotton short-sleeved shirt is still seen most frequently for the good reason that it's lightweight and looks neat. Furthermore, it's designed (as all good tennis shirts should be) so that the back is a few inches longer than the front; that way it doesn't become untucked when the wearer bends to scoop up a low shot. Another popular shirt is the collarless short-sleeved model of knitted polyester and cotton with navy and red stripes at neck and cuffs. But the newest and greatest tradition-toppler is the knitted white cotton tank top with skinny color trim.

When the breezes start to kick up, pull on a classic white cable-stitch, V-neck pullover sweater with navy and red border stripes. White shorts, of course, are preferred in cotton or cotton-polyester blend, and extend to a point approximately midway between hip and knee. A more avant-garde outfit: a white short-sleeved, short-leg zip-front jump suit of washable polyester-cotton mesh knit with navy belt and trim.

White athletic socks sometimes have a navy or red stripe at the top, but they *always* have a cushioned insole that serves to minimize the impact of running on the courts. As noted earlier, even the U.S. Davis Cup team in their yellow and blue outfits didn't tamper with their tennis sneakers; white canvas-tops are still *tops*. But snappiest new footwear seen on the courts is the leather oxford with nylon mesh inserts.

Sailing (Boating)

Here's another one of those sports popularly associated with the so-called privileged class, mainly, we suppose, because to the uninitiated, boat says *yacht*, and if it's a sailboat, visions of Kennedys sailing off Hyannis Port dance in their heads. So even if you're in hock to stay afloat, you'd best look affluent in a nicely offhanded style.

A hat isn't obligatory but some sort of headgear is advisable. In its casual way the white cotton hat with round crown and turned-down brim will do just fine, and so will a dark blue gabardine visor cap (perhaps with a yachting design in front).

A knitted cotton shirt, white or colored, in the T-shirt style, is highly recommended, along with white duck or washable slacks or shorts. (The white ducks look particularly fine when they have side stripes of navy.) For rougher weather wear a brightly colored or madras-printed nylon parka, specially processed for water-repellency; or a white terry knit pullover with navy stripes and a zipper shoulder closure.

Tennis socks are also boating socks. Tennis sneakers are also boating sneakers *except* on boats that have fine, highly polished decks. Then "top deck" shoes are in order. These look like tennis sneakers, but the soles are made differently; they're much more skid-resistant on wet decks, and at the same time they won't mark a shiny surface. You can get them in white or solid colors.

Swimming

Now, here's one sport that didn't start out as a plaything of the upper crust. Yet even though it strips you down, swimwear still manages to dress you up—particularly these days when swimsuits

SWIM SUITS

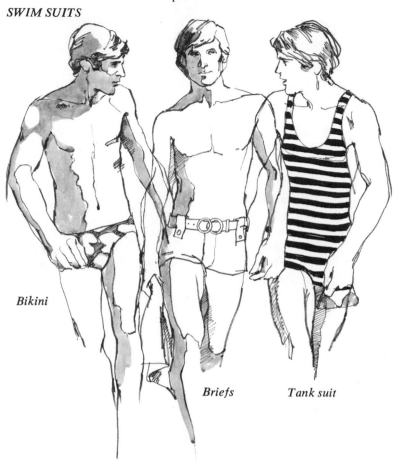

Bikini

Briefs *Tank suit*

offer such tremendous variety. Interesting, too, is the fact that as men's clothes—everything from suits to shirts to underwear—have become more figure hugging, swimsuits have taken on more fabric. An updated version of the turn-of-the-century tank suit, for instance, has won a big following, and that's meant fewer bare chests on the beaches.

Not every swimsuit is for every man, however, and since no sport displays quite so much of you, we'll take this opportunity to review some of the basic swimsuit styles. . . .

The really short trunks that rest on the hipbone and have square-cut legs were obviously designed with a lean young man in mind. And so were the 12-inch-long cotton duck trunks inspired by the hot pants of the distaff side. The swim-walk short modeled after the Bermuda walk short is well tailored and looks attractive on almost any man provided he's of at least average height. But the short man should avoid them, since their length tends to shorten the legs. Boxer-type shorts styled like the boxer underwear shorts are safe but, let's be truthful, *dull*.

The tank swimsuit or knit trunks worn with separate tank tops (usually barber pole striped) are vastly becoming. The bikini? If you don't have an extra ounce of flesh on your body and are a dyed-in-the-wool extrovert, why not?

Beach robes were big news in the thirties, but today's man prefers something more along the lines of a short-sleeved safari shirt; a three-tone tank top shirt; a short-sleeved knit pullover with a lace-up front; or a heavy canvas awning-striped sailing jacket. More avant-garde: a short satin jacket with diagonal zip pockets and snap front; or a caftan-inspired cotton robe that goes right down to the ankles.

Once you're out of the water, why not wear a hat? It's a good idea to protect face and head from the direct rays of the sun, and the big planter's-type straw beach hat is a dandy.

Sandals are plentiful. There are leather clogs with thick wooden soles and rubber strips to prevent slipping; leather-covered cork clogs with raised heel and toe platforms; leather boot-sandals; thong sandals; and laced sandals.

For walking on the beach or taking a turn around the boardwalk, consider a cotton knit sleeveless jump suit or a pair of striped cotton terry overalls.

Golf

For years now the conservative businessman has tossed inhibition to the winds every time he stepped out on the links, prompting *Esquire* some years ago to comment: "No sport permits its participants the freedom of imagination, the choice of colors and styles, and the opportunity to dress tastefully yet uniquely that golf does."

And that still holds true today—only more so.

Whether you wear a hat or not is entirely up to you. If you should decide to wear one, a cotton porkpie in a bright color would look properly casual . . . and so would a plaid round-crown cap with visor.

A knit pullover shirt with short sleeves goes well with a six-button, link-stitch or wide-rib knit cardigan of alpaca, lamb's wool or acrylic fibers. The pullover, like the tennis shirt, should have its tail longer in back to keep tucked in. And the cardigan most certainly should have a full-cut sleeve to allow for a free swing. An alternate for the cardigan might be a zipper-front golf jacket in a closely woven fabric of all cotton or cotton plus polyester that's been treated to be both water and stain repellent.

Your slacks can be any color you want but they should feel like a second skin. Which is why most serious golfers these days are wearing body-conforming knit slacks. In cool weather at the end of the season, knickers (wool or corduroy) and high wool socks are practical and stylish.

Golf shoes have spiked soles for sure footing, but once you're past that bit of cautionary styling, they have plenty of good looks going for them. The slip-on monks' shoe with strap-and-buckle closure over the instep is a popular style, especially in all white. Popular, too, are saddle shoes, and moccasins with bellows tongues and elasticized laces. Back in the twenties when the dressiest golfers wore knickers, golf hose attained fashion importance but today, with slacks, the golfer's socks are invariably just ribbed athletic socks in plain white or heather-blend wool. Not very inspiring but with so much color everywhere else in his outfit, it does make for a certain amount of contrast.

Sports-Car Driving

Anyone can be a sports car enthusiast. It's easy, and it doesn't cost anything. All you have to do is admire sports cars and wish you had one. Being a sports car driver is another matter. Jaguars don't grow on trees, and it seems that most people who take the trouble to own a sports car are also at pains to wear the appropriate clothes.

Just as there is a mute fraternalism within the community of sports car owners (blinking headlights at one another as they pass on the highway), there is also a certain *esprit* about their dress. And it starts on the head.

Headwear: Sports cars are of European origin, even if there are a few American makers now. So the hat (which is often all that shows) usually is reminiscent of this fact. The concealed-visor cap is very British; the patterned cloth hat reminds one of Rex Harrison and Professor Higgins, which qualifies; and the beret speaks for itself, as does the Tyrolean hat.

Torso: The turtleneck pullover sweater is a staple. A tweed or corduroy jacket with slanting pockets and deep vents—an adaptation of the informal horseback riding outfit. Over it all a "car coat," which is knee length (for free leg action), in camel's hair, soft suede leather, smooth cabretta leather, thick-set wale corduroy, polyester and cotton blend or tweed. A woolen scarf for brisk weather is a good touch. And soft pigskin gloves provide a sure, safe grip on the wheel.

Trousers: Trim-cut slacks in cavalry twill, corduroy, wool and, in rare instances, leather.

Footwear: Ribbed socks, any color to go with the rest of the outfit. Two-eyelet chukka boots with brushed-leather uppers and rubber soles. Or a bona fide driving shoe, which has a studded rubber sole extending over the heel and up the back of the shoe. This serves as a proper base for a man's foot when it's resting on the accelerator.

Horseback Riding

Another status sport, although the dude ranch did bring it down the social ladder a few notches. But there are two classes of riding: the formal, which is riding to the hounds, and the informal, for casual riding. Formal riding attire is called "riding pink," and this is one area where the Peacock Revolution hasn't made so much as a dent. Purists tend to regard those fashion rules as something akin to the Ten Commandments.

Riding-pink attire includes: A velvet reinforced cap or a high silk hat; a neckband shirt with white stock; a riding coat with flap chest pocket and flap pocket on one side at the waist seam; white string gloves; white riding breeches; and black dress riding boots with tan tops.

The following informal riding outfit is classic in style and may be used for fox hunting of an informal nature: A soft felt hat or bowler; an oxford or flannel shirt with striped rep or figured challis tie, or a turtleneck pullover and knit gloves with leather palms; a tweed riding coat with slanting pockets and deep center vent; tan riding breeches of stretch nylon and rayon twill with zipper leg fastener, zipper closure; tan riding boots.

Today, however, many of the younger horsemen are going in for much more informal togs when they're out for a casual canter. Blue denim pants, for example, worn with a jeans jacket with patch pockets, a work shirt in a faded blue cotton or wool, fancy Western boots and, if a hat is used, a wide-brimmed one.

Hunting

While hunting clothes don't carry the tradition of riding apparel, they do remain rather inflexible, less for the sake of tradition than for the fact that the rigors of the sport plus the climatic conditions impose certain restrictions on fabrics and styling. As a result, what the well-dressed hunter of the seventies wears is not all that different from what his father wore twenty or even thirty years ago.

Because there are other hunters who might mistake your footfall for that of a four-legged animal, the traditional red and black checked wool cap (or a bright crimson cap) should be worn to prove that you're human.

And since hunting seasons are generally in the fall, start out with thermal underwear. Over that a red and black plaid wool or blend shirt. Alternate shirt: bright crimson wool with two patch pockets. Coat of bright red wool with two lower patch pockets, two chest patch pockets and vertical side slits for hand warmers.

Wear bright red wool hunting pants or corduroy pants that can tuck into high boots and not get caught in the underbrush.

On your feet, 10- or 18-inch laced waterproof boots with cleated soles over knee-high thick wool socks. On your hands, hunting mitts with leather palm and free-trigger-finger construction.

Fishing (Trout)

The most contemplative of all sports requires no deep thinking on the matter of what to wear for it. Most of the outfit is either functionally necessary or traditionally sacred.

Moving from top to bottom: A traditional and practical round-crown processed-cotton hat with medium-width brim and air vents at the sides; brushed cotton or lightweight flannel tan shirt with long sleeves and two chest pockets; tan processed-fabric vest with zipper closure, multiple pockets for fly boxes and miscellaneous items and a piece of shearling at top to dry off flies; slacks of twill cotton in natural tan shade; waterproof rubber or rubberized fabric waders supported by suspenders. A chilly-weather alternate or supplement for the tan vest might be a zipper-front jacket with large patch pockets and close-fitting cuffs.

Bicycling

Blue chip tycoons, fashion models, young moms and dads and not-so-young moms and dads—they've all taken to their "wheels." A super body conditioner, the bicycle is also one sure way to weave through congested traffic and get where you want to go with a minimum of hassle. Now you can even tote your bike along with you when you travel by air; at least one airline has developed a "Bike Box" in which a touring or racing bicycle can be carried.

When you're using your bike as a means of locomotion, naturally you dress for the occasion you're riding toward. But when you're using your bike for pure sport, then you should dress for the sport. And not surprisingly, much of what you've got in your sportswear wardrobe will look stylish here and not a little of what you buy especially for bicycling will double for country and resort wear.

BICYCLE SHIRTS

*Tank-top cotton
pullover*

*Long-sleeve
cotton pullover
with crew neck*

When the weather's balmy, a body-hugging cotton pullover comes highly recommended. There are long-sleevers and half-sleevers with crew necks, and then there are the tank tops—any of which can also do double duty for beachwear. Some of these pullovers are in solid colors with the flag of the U.S., France, Britain or Italy (all great bicycling peoples) dressing up the chest. Others are emblazoned with multicolored horizontal stripes streaking across the chest and spilling over onto the sleeves.

Jean-style knit slacks that pick up one of the colors in the pullover are popular and for the by now obvious reason: devil-may-care knits move with you and are wonderfully comfortable when you're in motion.

A richly plaided short-sleeved stretch cotton shirt is another happy choice for warm-weather bicycling. And so is the ribbed acrylic knit with half sleeves. With the latter, a silk neckerchief tied with a double knot is a jaunty accessory.

When there's a nip in the air, pull on a wool pullover, or wear a cotton shirt and top it with a sleeveless sweater in a contrasting pattern. It could be a geometrically designed cotton shirt and a wavy-striped knitted acrylic sleeveless sweater.

Of course you can press your casual or unconstructed suit into service. A lanky stretch denim jump suit, for instance, is a dandy biking outfit.

When your wheels are snapping-crackling through a carpet of autumn leaves, it may be time to consider a ribbed turtleneck, a hefty suede belt, and tweed knickers tucked into suede boots. One of the sleekest bicycling outfits seen to date is the all-in-one knit knicker suit with suede belt and front suede patch pockets, worn with laced leather bike boots. Granted an outfit like that isn't for every man, but if you're trim enough and want an outfit that really says *bicycling,* this one is well worth the investment.

Most men like to speed along on their bikes sans head covering. But if you hanker to wear something on your head, there are the wide-brimmed straw hats for summer, and the checked and plaided caps for spring and fall. A glen plaid cap, for instance, tops off the all-in-one knit knicker suit with a maximum of style.

If you're the rugged type who'll continue to bike practically year 'round—just so long as it hasn't snowed—a wool shirt, a hefty sweater (perhaps one with a concealed hood), corduroy slacks and an honest-to-goodness beanie knitted in any number of non-wintry colors and pulled down over your ears, is an outfit that will work just fine in frosty weather. If the beanie is more than you bargained for, dip into your ski wardrobe and fish out a knitted wool cap or headband. Think twice before biking bareheaded in the frankly cold weather. Winter biking is rough.

As for footwear, anything goes just so long as it can grip the bike's pedals. As already noted, boots are dandy; leather ones for the cool days, and soft, cool white calf demiboots for the warmer days. Quite simply, you can slip your own pedal extremities into any footwear that captures your fancy: two-toned shoes with nicely squared heels and candy-striped laces; crepe-soled suedes with speckled laces; or perhaps a red-white-and-blue hard leather version of the classic sneaker, sporting a sponge sole. All high-spirited shoes for a high-flying sport.

KEEPING FIT

We defy any man—no matter how extensive his wardrobe—to look his best if he's overweight. Today's shaped suits and body shirts simply don't leave room for excess pounds. All of which dictates that you eat sensibly and exercise regularly to keep fit.

We Americans are a sports-loving people but we're also extremely gregarious. Result: we're team oriented. So when we leave the athletic fields of high school and college, too often we wind up watching sports events on television. No longer part of a team, we become spectators rather than doers. And if you don't think that's a tragedy, consider the dismal statistics regarding the average young American's physical fitness as measured by military service induction centers.

The following exercises are aimed at keeping you fit, so that you'll wear your clothes with the appropriate dash. They're a far cry from the weight-lifting kind of huff 'n' puff exercises, as indeed they should be. The bull neck and muscle-bound biceps are yesterday's ideal; they don't fit into today's clothes. Today's man is lean and smooth muscled, like a swimming ace.

Do these exercises every day; make them a habit like brushing your teeth. Before you dig in, however, always warm up first.

Warm-up Exercise

Stand with feet together and arms hanging relaxed at sides. Start hopping on left foot . . . switch to right foot . . . then back to left, continuing to hop this way throughout duration of this exercise. As you hop, swing both arms forward, up and back, making a complete circle. Do six complete circles of your arms.

For a Flatter Stomach

1. Lie perfectly flat on the floor, feet together and arms at your sides, palms down. Slowly raise both feet about 3 inches off the floor, at the same time raising your head just high enough to see your rising toes. Make certain not to raise your feet more than 3 or 4 inches. Hold this position for the count of 6. Return to starting position. Do six times.

2. Nice thing about this exercise is that you can do it at your office. Push your chair back from your desk to give yourself enough leg room. Extend both legs straight out, feet together on the floor. Slowly raise both feet to hip level, then slowly . . . very slowly . . . lower both feet until they're 3 or 4 inches above the floor. Hold this position for the count of 6. Return to starting position. Do six times.

For a Trimmer Waistline

1. Stand with feet apart, arms held horizontal and at shoulder level. Swing from the waist as far to the right as possible. Turn your head to follow the arm that is moved backward. Your arm should be pushed as far back as it can go without moving your feet. Return to starting position. Do ten times.

2. Sit on floor with legs spread wide apart, arms held horizontal and at shoulder level. Twist body from side to side, touching toes. This is a "toughie," so if you don't reach those toes the first few times, stick with it. Touching toes of both feet completes one cycle; do six times.

3. Sit on floor with legs spread wide apart, hands locked behind your head. Swivel, and with right elbow touch your left knee. Next, with left elbow touch your right knee. That completes one cycle; do six times.

Diet

Exercise alone isn't enough to keep you fit. After all, what good are a flat stomach and strong back if you feel blah? What you want is a strong, slender body packed with vitality, and that demands nourishing, nonfattening foods.

Statistics indicate that about 40 percent of our population is overweight, and chances are that a much larger proportion is chronically tired due to faulty diet. We're not going to use this space to veer off on a discussion of the vitamins you need and the foods that supply them (you should know them by now anyway, and if you don't there are plenty of good books on the subject). And if you're decidedly overweight, you should let your physician tell you the slimming diet best suited to your body and temperament. What we will do, however, is offer you the following commonsense tips on eating habits designed to keep your weight down and your energy up:

1. Eat three meals a day, concentrating on protein. The average man should have 20 grams of protein or the equivalent of three eggs (not fried) for breakfast. You'll be surprised how this protein eases the craving to eat something again before lunchtime. For lunch and dinner, eat lean meat or fish with whatever (nonfattening) foods you like. Just limit the portions.

2. Go easy on carbohydrates and fats generally, or reduce your portion intake. Translated this means you will avoid prepared breakfast cereals, bread, pastas, sweet wines, liqueurs, beer, jellies, jams, preserves, ice cream, cake, pies, candy, sugar, chestnuts, apricots, dates, bananas and potatoes, all rich in carbohydrates; and such fatty foods as duck, spareribs, sausages, bacon, whole milk, butter, cheese made from cream or whole milk, deep-fried snacks and puddings.

3. Substitute dry wine with meals for beer and liquor, which directly affect weight.

4. Change your eating habits. Substitute fruit for the pastry you think you can't live without.

5. Unsweetened grapefruit juice or quinine water before eating tends to dull the appetite if you're watching your weight.

6. Excessive use of salt leads to water retention, which adds weight. Use it sparingly.

7. Oysters, clams, leeks and raisins are energy foods, since they are a natural source of sodium.

8. Blue-pencil all pre-bedtime snacks. They're waistline poppers since when you're asleep you aren't actively burning up those calories.

CHAPTER TEN

Weddings and Formal
Evening Wear

Who Pays for What?

This may well be the last time you'll find yourself on the bargain side of the ledger. So enjoy it. For as the groom, your expenses are minimal compared to those of the bride's parents. As the husband —well, why go into that here and now? It's the wedding and preparations for the wedding that concern us at this moment, and here is how they're divvied up:

The bride's parents pay for:

Engagement announcements in the newspaper.

Wedding invitations and announcements.

Flowers for the church.

The fees for the sexton and the organist.

The bridesmaids' bouquets and presents.

The bride's wedding dress, clothes and linen.

All expenses of the reception: food, flowers, music, champagne and cars for the bridal party from the house to the church and from the church to the reception.

The groom pays for:

The engagement ring.

The wedding ring.

The marriage license.

The bride's bouquet.

The best man's and ushers' boutonnieres.

The ushers' presents, and their gloves and neckties.

The bachelor dinner.

136

The contribution to the clergyman (five dollars to five hundred dollars).

The automobile in which the bride and groom leave the reception.

All the expenses of the wedding trip.

Everything else in the regular course of a wedding.

What's Worn When?

It is significant that, despite the revolutionary changes that have taken place in men's fashions during the past several years, wedding attire has retained its status quo. To be sure, there have been a rash of weddings in which the bride and her groom have stood barefoot in a meadow while taking their marriage vows, but those ceremonies have been decidedly in the minority. And though many a freshly minted groom has been known to wear a jump suit and drive his bride off to their honeymoon hideaway on a motorcycle, when it comes to dressing for the wedding ceremony he usually bows in the direction of tradition. For here it is that tradition, cuffed around quite a bit in some other areas, still rules with little—very little—room for change. Therefore, you are herewith advised to honor and obey the following sartorial rules as they apply to the ceremony you are planning:

The Formal Daytime Wedding (Before 6 P.M.)

The purists insist on the following:

Coat. Black or oxford gray cutaway, with plain or bound edges; single-breasted with one or three buttons and peaked or notched lapels, or double-breasted, peaked-lapel model.

Trousers. Striped gray or striped black and gray, cuffless. Gray braces.

Shirt. White piqué with wing collar and stiff or pleated bosom.

Waistcoat. Single- or double-breasted to match coat, or light gray or buff (white is acceptable for summer).

Neckwear. Gray moiré striped or checked ascot, or gray-striped silk four-in-hand.

Shoes. Black straight-tip shoes, preferably a polished calfskin.

Socks. Black.

Hat (optional). High silk.

Jewelry. Pearl studs and cuff links with pearl tiepin (optional). Cuff links of gold, silver or semiprecious stones are acceptable but very definitely second choice.

Gloves. Gray, white or fawn mocha.

Outercoat. Black or oxford gray chesterfield with fly front.

Accessories. A plain white pocket handkerchief is optional, but a boutonniere is obligatory; white carnation, stephanotis or lily of the valley are correct. White or gray scarf.

Guests are expected to wear a similar outfit, although a dark business suit has become acceptable.

But today even the purists give the groom a little leeway, and in place of the cutaway, or morning coat as it's also called, a semiformal oxford gray or black walking coat—cut like a suit jacket—may be worn.

Still, since weddings are just about the last refuge for traditional formal wear, there is—as we've already noted—not a great deal of tolerance for change. Yet some slight changes have managed to squeak through and have brought with them a measure of comfort to what has always been a basically rather uncomfortable costume. The following outfit, for example, merits your attention for the fact that it takes the formal daytime wedding outfit and updates it without actually departing from tradition:

A shaped six-button double-breasted oxford gray morning coat with inset peaked lapels, deep flapped pockets and a really extravagant center vent; traditional-looking gray striped trousers of Dacron and worsted; a wing-collar shirt with French cuffs and a *soft* piqué bosom. The other appointments remain constant.

The Semiformal Daytime Wedding

Coat. Black or oxford gray jacket.

Trousers. Black and gray striped, cuffless. Gray braces.

Shirt. White pleated front with turned-down collar and French cuffs; or striped or solid-color shirt with a white stiff collar.

Waistcoat. Single- or double-breasted to match coat, or no waistcoat.

Neckwear. Gray-striped or checked silk four-in-hand.
Shoes. Black straight-tip, preferably polished calfskin.
Socks. Black.
Hat (optional). Black or midnight blue homburg. In summer, a sennit straw with formal-type band.
Jewelry. Gold or silver.
Gloves (optional). Gray mocha.
Outercoat. Black or oxford gray with fly front.
Accessories. White pocket handkerchief; white boutonniere; gray muffler.
Guests wear dark suits.

The Informal Day or Evening Wedding

Suit. Navy blue, black or oxford gray, single- or double-breasted. May be striped.
Shirt. White with attached collar and, preferably, French cuffs.
Waistcoat. Single-breasted to match jacket, or no waistcoat.
Neckwear. A conservative tie—small check, blue and white or black and white polka dot; gray or navy pincheck or pinstripe; solid navy.
Shoes. Black polished calfskin.
Socks. Black.
Hat (optional). Dark felt. In summer, a sennit straw with appropriate band.
Jewelry. Gold or silver.
Gloves (optional). Gray mocha.
Outercoat. Black, navy blue or oxford gray single-breasted woolen or worsted.
Accessories. Plain white pocket handkerchief; white boutonniere; gray or white scarf.
Guests wear dark business suits.

The Formal Evening Wedding (After 6 P.M.)

Coat. Black tailcoat.
Trousers. Matching the coat with a side stripe corresponding to the facings on the tailcoat lapels. Cuffless. White braces.

Shirt. White starched-bosom shirt with wing collar.

Waistcoat. Single-breasted white piqué.

Neckwear. Butterfly bow tie matching fabric of your waistcoat.

Shoes. Black patent leather lace-up fronts or pumps.

Socks. Black.

Hat. High silk.

Jewelry. Pearl studs and links.

Gloves. White kid, mocha or chamois.

Outercoat. Black single- or double-breasted dress coat.

Accessories. White pocket handkerchief; lily of the valley boutonniere; white silk scarf.

Guests are expected to wear white tie, although black tie is permissible.

The Semiformal Evening Wedding

Coat. Black or midnight blue tuxedo, with peaked lapels, shawl collar or satin-framed lapel.

Trousers. Matching coat. Cuffless. Black or white braces.

Shirt. White with tucked, pleated or ruffled front, as well as spread collar and French cuffs.

Waistcoat. Satin waistcoat or cummerbund to match coat. (Trousers with satin waistband are more and more eliminating the cummerbund.)

Neckwear. Satin butterfly bow to match coat.

Shoes. Black patent leather pumps or plain-tip oxfords.

Socks. Black.

Hat (optional). Midnight blue or black homburg.

Jewelry. Studs and links of smoked pearl, onyx or semiprecious stones set in gold or silver.

Gloves (optional). Gray or natural-color chamois.

Outercoat. Black, navy blue or dark gray chesterfield.

Accessories. White pocket handkerchief; red or white carnation; white scarf.

Guests wear dark jackets or dark suits.

The Summer Evening Formal Wedding

Coat. White single- or double-breasted dinner jacket.

Trousers. Black with satin stripe, cuffless. Black or white braces.

Shirt. Plain- or fancy-front formal, with spread collar and French cuffs.

Neckwear. Black butterfly bow (with matching cummerbund).

Shoes. Black, with plain toes.

Socks. Black.

Jewelry. Pearl studs and links.

Accessories. White pocket handkerchief; red carnation.

Guests wear light or dark dinner jackets.

The Summer Evening Semiformal Wedding

Coat. White single- or double-breasted dinner jacket, or black or midnight blue.

Trousers. Black or midnight blue. Black or white braces.

Shirt. White with tucked, pleated or ruffled front, as well as spread collar and French cuffs.

Neckwear. Black or midnight blue butterfly bow with the black or midnight blue dinner jacket; black, midnight blue or maroon with white dinner jacket. Cummerbund matches bow tie.

Shoes. Black, with plain toes.

Socks. Black.

Jewelry. Studs and links of smoked pearl, onyx or semiprecious stones set in gold or silver.

Accessories. White pocket handkerchief; red or white carnation.

Guests wear white or dark dinner jackets, or, if they wish, lightweight summer business suits.

The Garden Wedding

Coat. Navy blue, black, bluish gray or white single- or double-breasted jacket or blazer.

Trousers. White or gray flannel slacks.

Shirt. White dress shirt.

Neckwear. A conservatively striped or patterned tie (preferably in blue and white or gray and white). A burgundy-color tie also is attractive.

A Final Checklist for the Groom-to-Be

Be certain that when you buy a present for your bride, it's something for her personal adornment; nothing else is proper. It should be of an enduring quality in remembrance of this important event. Arrange to send her wedding flowers and a going-away corsage. Provide flowers for her and her mother. If the wedding is a formal day affair, it is customary that you provide ascot ties, stickpins, waistcoats and gloves for members of your wedding party; this is to ensure uniformity in appearance. This applies to the best man and the ushers. Your tie and the one for the best man should be of identical design, and all the ties for the ushers should match but be of another design. Don't forget to supply boutonnieres for the groomsmen, your father and prospective father-in-law. It's the practice today to sign the wedding license the day of the rehearsal. This will enable you to get to the reception as quickly as possible and will leave the wedding day uninterrupted by any "business" procedures.

In order that the wedding run smoothly, it is essential to understand that each step of the way, from the first day of planning, is established by tradition. An assortment of duties is assigned to you, the bride, the best man and the ushers, and above all there is the supreme law of protocol. Observe.

The Best Man

The bridegroom and his best man work out arrangements together from the time plans for the wedding are first started. The best man is usually the bridegroom's best friend or his brother. After discussion with the bridegroom, he helps in inviting the chief usher and ushers, making out the bridegroom's guest list, assisting in last-minute "things to be done" before the wedding, and generally acts as the bridegroom's representative.

One of his important duties is to organize arrangements for the chief usher and ushers. Just before the ceremony, he takes over the ring, gets the minister's fee from the bridegroom, helps the bridegroom dress and, above all, sees that the bridegroom gets to the wedding on time. In the meantime, he has checked travel, hotel and luggage arrangements, and seen that flowers sent by the bridegroom to his bride and her mother and grandmother (if there is one) are in order.

After the wedding he helps speed guests and attendants to the reception. He delivers the first toast to the bride and groom. When it's time for the newly married couple to leave the reception, he follows the bridegroom and sees him through changing, returning to his bride and getting away on schedule. After they leave, he sends a wire to the bride's parents, in the groom's name, thanking them for the reception.

Chief Usher

As his title implies, he is the supervisor and head man in charge of the ushers. He helps put the ushers through their paces at the wedding rehearsal. He should make himself familiar with seating arrangements and check the guest list to be sure that he knows members of the family, friends, special guests. He is the one who escorts the bride's and bridegroom's mothers to their respective seats and escorts both from the ceremony as well. He designates the duties of each usher, such as removing the aisle carpet covering in church and removing aisle ribbons. If there is confusion, or error in seating arrangements, he is the diplomatic arbiter.

Ushers

The chief duty of the ushers is to seat guests according to the seating plan.

The manner of the ushers should be friendly and quietly cordial. There should be a welcoming word for friends and acquaintances among the guests, but no prolonged conversational exchanges, as it's essential to get guests seated as quickly as possible to avoid delay and congestion in the aisle.

Ushers put up aisle ribbons and lay aside carpet covering before the processional, take part in processional and recessional, help remove the aisle ribbons. At the reception they attend unescorted ladies, mingle generally with the guests.

Bride's Father

Escorts daughter to processional. "Gives bride away" at the ceremony. Dances with daughter after the groom has done so. Acts as the host at the reception. Assumes financial responsibility for wedding, reception, transportation.

Bridegroom's Father

His only specific responsibility is to dance the third dance at the reception with his new daughter-in-law. And most important of all: the groom's father is just a guest at the reception. He should never try to take over any of the host's duties. That privilege belongs to the bride's father—after all, he's paying for it.

The Wedding

On the day of the wedding the best man helps the bridegroom dress for the ceremony—by that time, most grooms need all the help they can get. He also makes sure that the ushers are properly turned out. He sees to it that the ushers are at the church at least an hour before the time set for the ceremony, and gets the groom there at least twenty minutes early. He has custody of the ring. He arranges for the verger to hand the bridegroom and himself their hats and coats at the door of the church after the ceremony.

All female guests at the ceremony are escorted to their places by one of the ushers (there is usually one usher for every fifty guests —even if this results in more ushers than bridal attendants). When a couple arrives at the church, an usher greets them, offers the lady his right arm and escorts her up the aisle to a seat—her escort following along behind them, alone. If several ladies arrive together, the usher offers his arm to the oldest. Since the usher is the bridal couple's representative in greeting the guests, he is at all times friendly and cordial. During the walk up the aisle a few friendly remarks should be made about the weather or the decorations. This is done in a low voice, but never whispered.

The bride's guests are seated to the left of the church and the groom's guests to the right (right and left are determined from a position facing the altar). The head usher escorts the bride's mother and the mother of the groom to their respective places. (The bride's mother is the last person seated prior to the wedding procession and the first person escorted from the church after the wedding ceremony.) Once all the guests are seated, the ushers place a ribbon along the aisle side of their pews to make certain none leaves at the end before the wedding party does.

Enter the Bride

Immediately after the bride has entered the church and the organist starts the wedding march, the ushers, formed in a line of twos, march slowly up the aisle, about six feet apart. They are followed by the bridesmaids, the maid or matron of honor, the flower girl, if there is one, and then, about twelve feet behind her, the bride, who is on the right arm of her father. On the march from the chancel at the conclusion of the ceremony the bride takes the bridegroom's right arm. They are followed by the flower girl. The best man offers the maid of honor his right arm and escorts her from the church. Each usher escorts a bridesmaid from the church in the same manner. At the exit the ushers leave the wedding party; the head usher walks down the aisle and escorts the bride's mother from the church, followed by the father. He then returns and escorts the groom's mother from the church, the father following. The other ushers then escort the ladies among the special guests from the church. The ribbons which were tied from about the fourth pew (or however many pews were reserved for special guests) to the back of the church are then removed and the other guests leave the church.

The Reception

It's the responsibility of the best man to get all the wedding principals to the reception in good order so that the receiving line may form before the first guests arrive. The receiving line is usually formed just inside the entrance to the room where the reception is held. Since the wedding breakfast or reception is primarily a party, this room should be gaily decorated with flowers—not necessarily white. The bridal table, though, should be decorated with white flowers only.

If it is a large formal wedding, an announcer may be present. He asks the guests their names as they arrive and repeats them audibly to the bride's mother, who is first in line to greet the guests. Next to her stands the groom's mother, then the groom's father, then the bride and groom, then the maid of honor and the bridesmaids. The bride's father may stand in the receiving line between his wife and the groom's mother, but preferably he mingles with the guests as he would do at any party where he was host. Groomsmen never stand in the receiving line.

When the last guest has been received, the bride and groom take their places at the bridal table. If it is a large formal wedding, only members of the bridal party are seated at this table—and they are served this way even if everyone else is served buffet style.

The bride and groom sit facing the main room. The bride sits at the right of the groom, the best man at her right and the maid of honor at the groom's left. The bridesmaids and ushers are seated alternately around the table. Sometimes husbands of bridesmaids and wives of ushers are seated here, too.

As soon as the first course has been served, champagne is poured; the bride's glass is filled first, then the groom's, and then on around the table, ending with the best man. He then rises and proposes a toast to the bridal couple. After this toast the groom stands and thanks the guests.

After the main course has been served, the bride and groom cut the wedding cake, with both of their right hands on the knife together. Tradition demands that they share this first piece of cake as a symbol that they are ready to share each other's lives from then on. The guests are then served by the waiters.

Dancing

But this time the dancing, if there is any, should have started (and, if the wedding is large and formal, there should always be music—preferably an orchestra—whether there is to be dancing or not). The bride and groom always start the dancing—alone. Then, although others may share the floor after this, the bride's father cuts in on the groom, followed by the groom's father, the best man and each of the ushers. The groom dances his second dance with the bride's mother, then with his own mother. By now each of the bridesmaids has been partnered through her first dance by one of the ushers. After these formalities have been observed the dancing continues as at any party.

After a suitable time has passed and the bridal couple is ready to leave, the groom goes to a room that has been set aside for his use and changes to his travel clothes. The best man accompanies him and takes charge of his wedding clothes after he has made the change. The best man should have seen to it that everything was packed for the groom's wedding trip. He gets the newlyweds' luggage to the station or to their hotel—or at least sees to it that it's all safely stowed away in their car before they drive off.

That's the way it works at a perfect wedding. No one would want anything less, and that is why there are so many details of protocol to be observed. If one simply follows the rules, the whole thing will work without a hitch.

FORMAL EVENING WEAR

"And now no more, the rigid conformity that made one man in formal evening clothes look pretty much like every other man in formal evening clothes," observed *Esquire* in 1968. Permissiveness, after all, was one of the pleasantest and most persuasive points of the fashion revolution, and one of the legacies it left us is that these evenings a man dressing for an after-six formal can, if he wishes, show lots of color—in short, be more a peacock than a penguin. He can, that is, if the occasion doesn't dictate "white tie." When it does, *tradition* still holds. So on those relatively few "white tie" occasions such as debutante parties, benefit dinners, balls and official public affairs, these are the hard and fast rules that must be observed:

Coat. Either black or midnight blue. And incidentally, this is a prime example of the new permissiveness, since once upon a time in the not too distant past it was black and only black that counted. Satin or grosgrain silk facings on lapels are acceptable.

Trousers. Same fabric as coat, with a single pleat or no pleats at all at the waistband, and single or double braids set closely at both outer side seams.

Waistcoat. Either single- or double-breasted white piqué is correct.

Shirt. White piqué bosom (no longer stiff) with link cuffs and attached wing collar (no longer starched).

Neckwear. White piqué butterfly bow.

Shoes. Black patent leather. There are some mavericks who have taken to black calfskin, but the purists dictate patent leather. You do, however, have some leeway in choosing the style of your shoe. It may be a pump, a laced bal front style or a slip-on.

Socks. Over-the-calf silk or nylon. Black or midnight blue depending on your tailcoat. Lightweight wool, lisle or a flat-ribbed knit are also acceptable. And if you wear garters, make sure they're *white.*

Hat (optional). High silk.

Jewelry. White pearl or semiprecious stone. (Once upon a time, only a pocket watch could accompany a tailcoat but today a wristwatch is acceptable, although a black leather or suede band is heartily recommended.)

Gloves. White kid, mocha or chamois. Kid is the favorite, but chamois is washable.

Overcoat. Black chesterfield with black collar. Actually, any black coat of a more formal fabric and design is correct for wear with tailcoat. The black cape with velvet collar has made a comeback, and many a man is partial to its special brand of dash.

Accessories. A white pocket handkerchief, preferably silk, and arranged to show multiple points. A white or red carnation on the jacket lapel. A knitted or woven white silk scarf around your neck if the weather calls for it. (Some men like an embroidered monogram on theirs, but that's begun to look rather ostentatious.)

NOTE: Tails of the tailcoat should extend no more than a fraction of an inch below the bend of the knee in back. In front, the tailcoat should come below the natural waistline so that no part of your waistcoat extends below it. Sleeves should be tapered with an inch of shirt cuff showing.

Semiformal Evening Dress

Still designated as "black tie," although here is where the peacock finally gets his chance to strut. All the rules haven't been broken, but they most certainly have been bent, as you'll see from the following list of alternatives to the once strictly black and white uniform look:

Coat. Black and midnight blue still dominate the months from September to May, but a lush dark brown is today in third place. Mohair and worsted were usually the favorite choice during these months, but now you may wear a velvet or a double knit. One of the smartest-looking dinner jackets to come along in years is the cotton velvet with the super-size paisley pattern and black velvet lapels. Clearly, if you go formal often this is a second jacket (after all, how much paisley could you stand night after night?). So if you must have velvet and it will be your sole dinner jacket, skip the paisley and settle for a solid burgundy velvet.

As far as summer formal wear goes, who says you must confine yourself to a white dinner jacket? Today pastels, stripes and vibrant colors are all acceptable. To demonstrate just how far semiformal evening dress for the summer months has been liberated, the following dinner jackets are being seen at the most fashionable resorts: a peacock blue denim with black velvet lapels; a pink double knit with burgundy velvet lapels; and an off white with pink and blue prism stripes and black satin lapels.

Should your coat be single- or double-breasted? It's strictly up to you. Even here the revolution has made itself felt; a single-breasted dj, for instance, may now have as many as four satin-covered buttons or *no buttons at all* if the jacket is cardigan-style.

Trousers. They're usually black or dark blue and usually of the same fabric as your dinner jacket. But not necessarily. Furthermore, since 1970 we've seen everything from windowpane checks to plaids and tapestried paisley designs crop up in trousers for spring-summer black tie wear. In short, the choice is now wide open but a wise man will inevitably choose carefully, bearing in mind that the extreme fashion all too often carries its own built-in obsolescence. So if your spring-summer dinner jacket is colorful, we suggest you wear dark trousers with it. Or buy a midnight blue or black tuxedo and then, for variety's sake, an extra pair of more colorful trousers.

Waistcoat. Or cummerbund. The choice is purely personal. At one time the cummerbund was restricted to wear with your summer dj, but today it's a year-round item. The waistcoat is dressier than the cummerbund and especially so when it's black. The cummerbund in silk or faille has a special appeal, however, since it can be worn in a color to match your bow tie.

Shirt. Pleated, tucked or ruffle-front formal with turned-down collar and French cuffs. Varied shades of blue have become increasingly popular and, to a lesser extent, some other colors in pastel hues. One particular standout is the white ruffled shirt (even the cuffs are neatly ruffled) with all the ruffles edged in black.

Neckwear. In fall and winter, black or midnight blue bow tie depending on your dinner jacket. In summer all that's asked is that the bow match the waistcoat or cummerbund. Maroon, the first to break the color barrier, is most frequently seen.

Satin is still the favorite, but velvet has gained considerable ground. The butterfly shape still dominates and some of the butterflies have inflated to extravagant widths, but unless you're in a mood to collect a wardrobe of formal bow ties, you'd do well to choose one of more moderate proportions. (If you're all thumbs, a clip-on is advised. They've been so perfected that only you will know you didn't tie it yourself.) Tip: the straight-end bow tie is always in style.

Shoes. Black patent leather and polished calfskin still head the list, although brown patent leather or suede is more compatible with a dark brown dinner suit. The late sixties saw the debut of colored formal footwear, but the plain-toe black shoe not only survived but thrived.

The pump with black dull-ribbed silk bow, correct with both tailcoat and dinner jacket, is a wise investment, and so is the two-eyelet patent leather oxford, for the same reason. Further down the list is the plain-toe leather oxford, acceptable but, let's face it, not excessively stylish.

Socks. Black, or a deep shade of brown if the dinner suit is brown. (Years ago actor Van Johnson wore fireman red woolen socks with his black tuxedo, but the fad started and stopped with him.)

Hat (*optional*). The black or midnight blue homburg. You don't often see a man wearing a high silk or opera hat with a dinner jacket, but it's correct nonetheless. For summertime, you might wear a coconut palm with a white linen band. (The same hat with a madras band would be all wrong.)

Jewelry. Smoked or black pearl, black onyx, gold or semi-precious stones. The latter are seen mostly in dark blue or dark red.

Gloves. Gray mocha, chamois or buck, button or slip-on style.

Overcoat. A black or dark blue of a formal fabric or design (e.g., the chesterfield).

Accessories. The color of your pocket handkerchief depends on the color of your dinner jacket. If your jacket is blue or midnight blue, you may have a handkerchief in anything from white to a solid color or a paisley. If your summer dj is white, your pocket handkerchief should match your bow tie or at least be in a compatible color. If you've chosen a brocade dj or one with a tapestry effect, you'd do well to skip a pocket handkerchief altogether, but if you think that would leave you feeling seminude, make certain your handkerchief is in a subdued solid color.

Your scarf should be white, black or pale gray.

A white or red carnation is proper, but if your outfit is particularly colorful, you might skip the boutonniere or run the risk of looking like an ambulatory Christmas tree.

The Velvet Suit. This is increasing in popularity and deserves some special consideration here, since it brings with it a new set of fashion guidelines.

Certainly if you choose to wear a velvet dinner suit, it should be in a subdued shade like deep brown, navy, deep green or maroon. Your butterfly bow tie should then be in a deep shade harmonious to your suit and your socks should be of a deep solid color—either black or color-keyed to your suit. Your shoes should be patent leather or have a similarly formal look in a color compatible with your suit. Shirt and jewelry should be the same as what you'd wear with a conventional tuxedo.

CHAPTER ELEVEN

Accessories

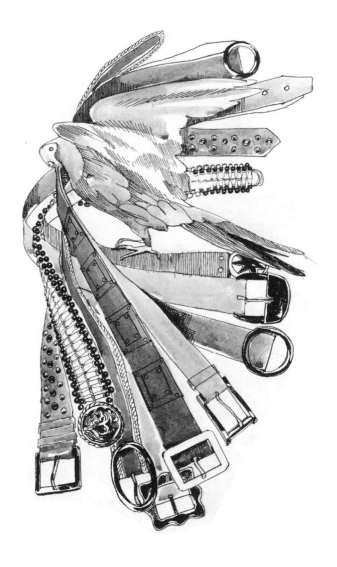

JEWELRY

For generations the American man has been circumspect with regard to his jewelry. So circumspect, in fact, that he'd rarely refer to it as "jewelry." As a result his cuff links, tie tacks and bars, et cetera, have been neat and functional and little else. Then along came the Peacock Revolution and many a man who was a lame duck in the jewelry department suddenly became an overt peacock. And at last jewelry, like aromatics, took its rightful place in the American man's scheme of things.

Today any man with a claim to being *au courant* regards jewelry as an essential accessory for the good life—a healthy expression of the male ego. And now his cuff links, tie tacks and bars, bracelets, rings, pendants, watches and even watch straps are sheltered under the heading of Jewelry.

Exactly how many French-cuffed shirts you own is a matter of personal preference, but certainly you should have some if only to give you an opportunity to show off a handsome pair of cuff links. Of course, the cuff links of gold, silver or semiprecious stone you have for formal or semiformal daytime occasions *could* lead a double life, but that would be a downright shame since there are so many links that while not correct for formal or semiformal wear are super with daytime dress shirts. The enameled and miniature mosaic links, for instance. And for a more restrained look, the gold or gold-plated, silver or silver-plated coins and button effects. (One rule to remember: never mix your metals. It's all silver or all gold.)

The size of your jewelry should always be in scale with your

girth and height. Certainly a man with a smallish hand, for example, should avoid a cuff link that's on the massive side and he'd also do well to confine himself to a small-scale tie tack or bar, even during those wide-tie periods when tacks and bars take on more heroic proportions.

If you are still wearing your class ring, we suggest it's high time you stowed it away with your graduating class photograph and moved on to more exciting jewelry. Here you must of course take into consideration the shape of your hand before settling on a ring. The slim hand with tapered fingers can't carry the same stylish heft a broad, blunt-fingered hand can.

The ID bracelet or "dog tag" of World War II took the curse off bracelets for men. So if you're in a mood to dress up your wrist, there are any number of tasteful interpretations of the ID bracelet to choose from.

Pendants as a class of body jewelry have suffered from over-exposure, having rattled on the scene along with the much publicized but short-lived Nehru dinner jacket. Still, a pendant often looks handsome accompanying a casual suit or a colorful beach outfit. It is, however, essentially the property of the fashion extrovert.

As for wristwatches and their straps, the Peacock Revolution has done just about everything but reworked the inner springs in the name of fashion. The face of a watch today has as many shapes as the human face, and straps, which were once a ho-hum brown or black, are now available in luscious shades of leather and suede, not to mention the handsome and pliable mesh straps that are to today's watches what knits are to suits.

If the new, personality jewelry attracts you but you still haven't indulged, it's time you did. Simply start slowly and feel your way along. Take your time . . . ponder your selections . . . and then wear them with aplomb.

GLASSES

Like everything else you wear, eyeglasses—once strictly utilitarian —have become fashion accessories. High time, too. After all, the specs through which you look out at the world should tell the world something about you. So whether your glasses are for peering at print or glaring back at the sun, they should reflect your outlook on life.

Here are some guidelines to follow when selecting your eyeglass frames:

If your face is round, choose a pair of sharp-cornered frames to offset the circular sweep of your facial contours.

If your face is long and/or thin, naturally you want to suggest a rounder look. You should choose frames that are more ringlike, but not too heavy.

If your face is small, steer clear of the king-size or heavy frames.

If your nose is longer than you'd like it to be, a low-bridge frame will appear to snip off some of its length.

If your nose is shorter than you'd like it to be, select a high-bridge frame that will expose every fraction of an inch.

If you feel the lines around your eyes are adding years to your appearance, invest in frames that are sturdy-looking enough to

EYEGLASSES

act as camouflage—dark plastics that have the tortoiseshell look, for instance. (Avoid genuine tortoiseshell; it's brittle and as a result is easy to crack.)

Rimless glasses have been out of favor for so long, they're due for a comeback and for two very good reasons: (1) trend-setting European students have taken them up and they've caught on in Paris, and (2) rimless specs are especially becoming with the longer men's hair styles. So if you have a penchant to go rimless— and they look well on you—*go*.

Popular for the same long-haired reason are the colonial or

so-called granny glasses with their skinny wire rims—a style worn by such diverse types as John Lennon, Woodrow Wilson, Sigmund Freud and Dustin Hoffman.

But the biggest splash in specs in the seventies has been the revival of the big models worn by Air Force aces of World War II —those giant teardrop or kidney-shaped affairs with a sweatband sometimes supported by a metal ring or O. A fashion savant wouldn't be caught without the lenses of his aviator's glasses tinted, say, an ice blue or green or amber shade. It would appear that the motorcycle cultists of the late sixties (epitomized by Peter Fonda in *Easy Rider*) sparked the revival of these old favorites and then they were taken up by everybody from rock musicians and male models to such clearly cerebral types as Norman Mailer, James Baldwin, James Jones and glamorous Women's Lib activist Gloria Steinem.

All of which makes the question of the color of your eyeglass frames seem nonstrategic. Well, there was a time when men were advised to take into consideration their hair color and complexion shade when selecting frames. But today—assuming your glasses have frames that will take color—that's not the way to do it. Now you choose the color frame you think looks best on you and that's that.

What tint should the lenses of your sunglasses be? (No need, we think, to go into the fact that eye-appealing sunglasses have become so *status* that many a man wears them even when there's no sunshine.) Yellow and amber are immensely popular, perhaps because they appear to douse the world you look out on with happy color, and furthermore they have status since the shooting glasses worn by the landed gentry in Scotland boast lenses tinted yellow. However, the very darkest colors offer 75 percent screening protection from harmful rays of the sun, while the lightest colors screen out a meager 45 percent of those rays. Still, a true-color gray is a top favorite via a polarized lens that is nearly clear indoors but gets progressively darker outside, depending on the brightness of the sun.

A couple of years ago, bottle blue and garnet red lenses were introduced and promptly taken up by the most fashion-conscious femmes. More recently some of the more extroverted men have begun to wear them, too, but if you limit yourself to a single pair of sunglasses, we think you'd grow weary of viewing a blue- or red-tinted vista no matter how extroverted you may be. But then we don't think any really well-turned-out male—extrovert or intro-vert—should limit himself to a single pair of sunglasses.

One last note: if you're an active sportsman, you should look into the sunglasses specially designed for specific sports. For shooting and fishing, for instance, there are glasses with large, deep-curve lenses that will protect your vision from all angles. And for the contact sports there are wire-rimmed pairs, and for golf bifocals with a tiny short-focus spot just big enough to read the score card with and small enough to leave the rest of the visual field clear.

BELTS AND SUSPENDERS

The shapelier clothes became, the bigger, bolder and brassier belts became. *Esquire* summed it up when it noted: "What counts now is to have the biggest belt on the block." But if you were a boutique shopper—a bona fide member of the jeans generation—a hand-made look was what counted most.

Still, belts, like some waistlines, have a tendency to narrow or widen with the seasons. Furthermore, every man isn't built for or temperamentally suited to the big *super*belts that clash with a waistline that's seen too many cream sauces and too little exercise, or with a personality that's basically conservative at heart. But no man has to settle for a "safe" belt. Happily, there are exciting belts available in a great variety of styles and widths. Invest in a belt wardrobe, and we suggest you build yours along the following lines:

Sportswear

Consider a leather, perhaps patent leather, with hardware trim or nailheads. (An unbuttoned cardigan sweater will allow you to show the most important part of your belt without revealing all of you in the round.)

Business

Something more conservative is asked for here, but it's still a far cry from the almost strictly functional belts of a few years ago. In fact, what with the assortment of leathers in offbeat shades and featuring extraordinary buckles, a belt that sits at the executive conference table can lead a double life on easygoing weekends. A black belt, for instance, with multicolored rows of stitching; a black or brown leather with a colored suede panel; a natural suede with a filigree buckle.

Jeans

Under this classification we include the vest suit, the shirt suit— in other words, *all* the nonsuits that reveal the waistline without the cover of a conventionally styled jacket. And here it would be folly to settle for anything less than one of the aggressive, look-at-me type belts. So if you're game for one of the casual suits, investigate the two-tone leathers clenched with large chrome buckles; the wide gold-mesh numbers; the hand crochets; and the husky cowhides featuring antique-brass harness bits.

With belts so popular these days, some department stores and men's specialty shops have added belt boutiques. And you rarely find belts displayed anywhere in boxes; they're hanging out where they invite close inspection and plenty of tactile communication. So you have only yourself to blame if you don't pick up a belt with a true seventies personality.

As for *suspenders,* what can we say? There was a time when a man ordering a suit from his tailor invariably had buttons put on the trousers for his suspenders, along with loops for his belt—and if he was a play-it-safe type he very often wore both simultaneously. Perhaps the vogue for novelty suspenders decorated with bubble-shaped gay nineties cuties and acrobats with handlebar mustaches helped to do in suspenders, along with the fact that as fashions grew shapelier and men more figure conscious, suspenders were just too much of an undercover item to survive. As a result, as belts have soared, suspenders have sagged. Until they stage a comeback (and they're bound to), the only suspenders you need concern yourself with are the all-white or all-black ones your formal evening attire demands.

HANDKERCHIEFS

Except for the time of a severe head cold when no man can ever carry enough handkerchiefs on his person, paper tissues in a plastic envelope are an affront to good taste. Simply because the functional handkerchief—or, if you will, the handkerchief for blow— is invisible most of the time is no reason for you to give it short shrift. Such a useful accessory offers you a splendid opportunity to establish your fashion credentials. So you are hereby urged, and *strongly,* to make absolutely certain that in your trouser pocket you always carry a handsome white hand-rolled handkerchief of quiet distinction. The people who count will notice.

As for the pocket handkerchief, that's strictly for show and has been ever since the Prince of Wales endorsed the fad of the bright silk pocket handkerchief back in the roaring twenties. One of the marks of the man who really has a bit more dash to his wardrobe is his choice of this breast pocket accessory. You can of course put in a white handkerchief (it's always correct and is obligatory for formal attire), but you'll find that the little extra effort involved in selecting a colored cotton or silk is well worth it. When you flip some color into your heart pocket, it not only gives a lift to your appearance but it also usually has a buoyant effect on the people you come face to face with.

While your pocket handkerchief should bear a filial relationship to the colors of your shirt and tie, it must never be a direct match either in color or pattern. When you choose a patterned square, don't fear boldness. Just take care that the pattern picks up a color from either your shirt or your tie. You're not striving for a match but rather for a happy look of color harmony. Patterns may also be mixed—as for example a small checked silk square and a striped tie—provided the shirt is a solid color. But mixing patterns is tricky, and when in doubt, tuck in a solid-color square and *know* you're correct.

There is, of course, more than one way to insert a pocket handkerchief but only one that really counts. The triangle fold is too studied; the pointed style with several points showing is correct for formal attire and too formal otherwise; and the straight fold revealing just a narrow band of handkerchief went by the boards along with the big dance bands. All of which leaves the *puff,* which looks smartly casual for the good reason that it is. And how can it fail to look that way when all you do is take all four corners of the square . . . shake . . . fold in half and insert in your breast pocket?

NECKERCHIEFS

The neckerchief does wonders for smartening up the collar of your sport shirt and looks properly dashing when worn with a sports jacket (especially a blazer). It should therefore figure prominently in your sports wardrobe. If for some reason you don't want to invest in a neckerchief, you can use a simple silk square, but make it at least a 30-inch one so you have something to work with.

There are two ways to tie your neckerchief: the ascot and the double knot. The former is achieved via the simple route of draping one end over the other. The double knot is exactly that and makes for a more casual effect and a more secure knot, looking especially well with a round-neck sweater or polo shirt.

SCARVES

We all know what to do with a scarf. You tie it around your neck when you're cold. It's a good way not to get a sore throat. But beyond this basic, there are some subtleties. The way you tie or knot your scarf, for instance.

Just wearing it tucked under the lapels of your overcoat or topcoat is adequate, but don't be afraid *not* to wear it that way. Tie it ascot style: just drape one end over the other. The effect is ultrasmart, ultraneat, ultrasnug. And if you're wearing a scarf of a brightly colored wool, and it's long enough and you're young enough, why not wrap it once around your neck, toss the longest end over your shoulder and let it hang free?

NECKWEAR

Double-knot neckerchief

Ascot neckerchief

Of course, no one scarf will work with every outfit. Silk, for instance, is more formal than wool (and not as warm). Plaid or checked wool is less formal than a solid color and the least formal of all is your old school six-footer. Your plaid and checked wool scarves belong with your suburban and sports jacket wardrobe. They shouldn't be bulging below the collar of a dressy overcoat or topcoat.

For evening you'll want white or at least black, dark blue or dark gray.

COSMETICS
AND TOILETRIES

GROOMING AIDS

The day when a splash of aftershave, a dab of talc and a deodorant made up a man's toilet faded away with the crew cut. Today not one area of the male body need go unattended.

Exactly how much you may care to invest in grooming aids is of course a matter of personal preference, but certainly you should know something about what is available and what it can do for you. For instance . . .

Cologne

You may call it toilet water if you prefer, but as time marches on the more stylish-sounding designation of *cologne* is used most often. But no matter what you call it, a cologne is a fragrant "water" containing more alcohol and more perfume than an aftershave lotion. It isn't meant to replace your aftershave, which is created to close your pores and soothe your skin after shaving. Cologne, on the other hand, is created to make you smell good and, in a very real sense, make you feel good about yourself, too. It can and should be used for more than just splashing on the face: as a body rub after your shower and for dabbing on your pocket handkerchief or on the shoulders of your dress shirt.

Cologne may be derived from any one of six basic aromas—wood, citrus, flowers, leather, spices and tobacco—and its scent will last longer than that of your aftershave. One of the most important tips we can give you regarding your choice of cologne and aftershave lotion is that they should be compatible—in other words, their scents shouldn't do battle for supremacy; and the very best way to assure their compatibility is to choose them from the same maker and, as a result, both will have been derived from the same basic aroma.

Perfume

As one wag put it, perfume is to cologne what Cadillac is to Chevrolet. Or more simply, the more potent perfume is part of a whole way of life. Question is, are *you* ready for it? If you are, men's perfume comes in regular spray bottles and can be had in a pocket-size container.

Pour Le Bath

Now that men have come right out and admitted their sexuality via the new wave clothes and personality haircuts, they're getting down to the nitty-gritty of it all and putting some masculine glamour in their bath water via lightly scented gels and liquids that not only help them get clean, but also help them relax in a truly luxurious way. Most if not all of these so-called soaps are not confined to bathtub only, but may also be used on a washcloth or sponge ·in the shower. And usually they contain emollients and conditioners which make the skin feel more refreshed.

Here the choice should be determined by your skin type. There are, for example, soaps specially formulated for problematic dry skin.

Personal Deodorant Spray

Underarms aren't the only spots prey to perspiration. So now there are the genital sprays, unscented and handsomely packaged.

Skin Bronzers

And they do exactly what this categorical name suggests, "toasting" your fagged-out complexion to a healthy, just-back-from-Barbados bronze. Actually you have a choice of just how native you want to look, since the skin bronzers come in light, medium and dark shades. The skin bronzer is packaged in a handsome plastic tube, and a few dabs on a fingertip will do the job on face and neck (and don't forget the *back* of your neck). And since you'll probably use your bronzer after you have your shirt on, be sure to slip a towel or a few tissues into the collar. (Bronzers don't stain except during the first few seconds just after application. After that, staining is no problem and in fact only soap and water rubbing will remove your tan.)

Facial Masques

Women have been using them for generations, to clean, refine and firm their skins, and now masques are being used by men who are convinced that with today's polluted air, soap-and-water-clean really isn't clean enough. Usually in the form of a clear gel, the masque is applied with the fingertips directly to face and neck, where it instantly forms a tight, latexlike film. After about fifteen minutes, it comes off via peeling or is washed off with warm water.

For the Head

Ever since big-name athletes went on television to advertise the fact that they used hair spray, and media-wise, youth-conscious politicos started dyeing their hair, there's been a positive boom in hair products for men. And since we've all become practically obsessed with hair as a way of looking young and contemporary, there is a plethora of protein products from shampoos to hair dressings whose purpose is to make thin hair look thicker and fuller. And if a man wants to go a giant step further in that direction, there are *hairpieces* of human hair or synthetic materials.

Today you can buy a truly first-rate hairpiece in any kind of hair style you want, long or short. The very best are constructed with lace bases which allow the scalp to show through in the right places.

While genuine human hair sounds preferable to the synthetic variety and is much more expensive, be advised that human hair fades and discolors. And furthermore, the upkeep is steeper. Small wonder synthetic hair like synthetic fur is fast gaining ground.

Still, some men are hairpiece shy and prefer something that seems to be more permanent. Like *hairweaving,* for instance. Quite simply, this is the weaving of foreign hair to what's left of your own hair. And here's how it's done:

A couple of strands of braided nylon thread are stretched across the thin or balding area, then crocheted onto the hairs at the border of your remaining denser growth. This serves as the foundation on which new hair is attached—permanently. The newly woven hair is styled like and looks like your own. And you treat it like your own. You comb it. You sleep in it, even swim in it.

Any minuses? A few. For example, as your hair grows, the foundations must be tightened every six weeks or so for about twenty-five dollars each time. Furthermore, some men complain that they don't like the fact that they can't clean the scalp beneath the weaves.

Hair implantation is another technique used to custom fit hair to your head permanently. Only this way it's done surgically:

plastic or Teflon-coated wires are actually sutured into your scalp, and sections of these implants are left exposed on your head in order to work as anchors to which a hairpiece is attached. Sure there's some blood shed and of course it takes time and money (over a thousand) to complete the whole implantation. In short, it's not something you rush into.

Hair transplants are, as the name suggests, a way of transplanting hair, by removing small plugs of hair-growing skin from so-called fringe areas and "planting" them in a bald area via a special surgical punch. Enough transplants are made this way to produce a reasonably dense hair growth. Scabs formed by dried blood serve as the anchor that holds the plug of transplanted hair in place until it heals. (During the healing process the transplanted hair breaks off, but when healing is accomplished the hair re-emerges and continues growing.)

For the man who really wants something *permanent,* this is it. His own hair sprouting out of what was once a bald spot. But— and it's a big *but*—this process is sometimes quite painful and always costly (say, twenty-five dollars or more per plug), and while the plugs are healing your scalp usually looks fairly scabby. Yet after about six weeks (more or less, since it depends on how bald you are and how fast the doctor wants to plug), you've got *hair!*

Certainly no one but a doctor should do a hair transplant, and if you don't know one who does, you can get a list of doctors who do from the American Medical Association or your local medical group.

As it is, we've only scratched the surface of the range of grooming aids designed to make you a smoother-skinned, fresher-smelling, healthier-looking male animal. A visit to a department store or a well-stocked drugstore will fill in the gaps and, furthermore, in many instances you'll come face to face with a representative of one of the companies putting out these products, who'll be able to answer questions and more than a little willing to demonstrate some of the products for you.

CHAPTER TWELVE

Travel

LEATHER GOODS AND LUGGAGE

Among the more glaring examples of personal sabotage a man can indulge in is the sorry-looking wallet. It belongs right up there near the top of the list along with run-down heels, stained tie knots and scruffy-looking luggage. A wallet is a clue to a man's degree of self-esteem. Not that the money clip is off limits, but it simply doesn't have the panache of a wallet that appeals to both the hand and the eye.

A wallet should be skinny. No matter how rich you are, never stuff your wallet out of shape. If you must carry a lot of cash, have it in bills of large denominations. And if your credit cards are many, we suggest you keep them not in your wallet but in a special, equally handsome credit card case of a matching leather.

Certainly your choice of leather is wide: pinseal, calfskin, pigskin, ostrich, et cetera. The skins of reptiles are, as you know, mostly taboo during this era of ecological awareness; however, new embossing techniques make it possible to permit any kind of texture to be placed on cowhide to simulate the exotic reptilian patterns.

Regardless of what your wallet is made of, be certain that its corners are reinforced with slim bands of brass. Many wallets come already reinforced, but if yours isn't, ask to have it done before you take it out of the store. These decorative-looking bits of brass will add immeasurably to the life-span of your wallet.

It should go without saying that for formal or semiformal evening wear your wallet should be black. An understated pinseal or calfskin is preferred, and silk, though handsome, is rarely if ever seen anymore.

The coming of the shaped suit presented a problem for many

men who found they had little room in their pockets for the gear they had to tote around with them every day. In some instances that even included the indispensable wallet. And rather than spoil the lines of the suit with unsightly bulges, some men took to the shoulder bag as a practical solution to the problem of the bulging pocket. Most of the truly status stores across the country began selling them in leather, suede and even llama, while the less adventurous man resorted to carrying a slim leather envelope that resembled a miniature attaché case.

Naturally, there were the usual self-conscious jokes about men carrying handbags, and to counteract the snickers some manufacturers took to promoting their styles with "muscular" copy along the lines of "The man's shoulder bag that's all man." *Esquire* dubbed some of the newest models "miracles of convenience, compartmented in such a way as to make them essentially portable desks and file folders."

Is a shoulder bag *your* bag? Only you can answer that one. But whatever your answer, don't let fear of being stared at influence your decision. If you really feel you need one, get one.

And if you're a man who travels to any extent, you certainly should consider a permanent travel kit for your grooming aids. A leather one would be a fine luxury, but today,the largest selection appears to be in the vinyls. In either case, they're compact, with zipper lids and flat sides, and take up an absolute minimum amount of space in your luggage. And if you travel a great deal, we suggest you maintain a permanent kit with everything prepacked and ready to go. Basically, here's what should be included in the well-stocked case: razor and package of blades; shaving foam or cream; aftershave; talcum and powder puff for it; toothbrush (in a case) and paste; aspirin; comb (unbreakable); deodorant; shampoo, hair groom or spray (if used); toe and fingernail clippers; styptic pencil; bandages (one of each size); two collar stays.

The above items may not fit into a case in their regular sizes, so be sure to buy the smallest sizes of everything.

We previously mentioned scruffy-looking luggage and sorry-looking wallets as two examples of personal sabotage. So we don't really have to belabor the point any further; handsome luggage is absolutely essential to a well-turned-out appearance. And since packing a bag is rarely any man's idea of a good time, you should help alleviate some of the annoyance by (1) selecting the proper size luggage so as to make packing as simple as possible, and (2) learning a little something about how to pack.

Now, if you're only going on a two-day business trip, you don't need a huge suitcase that you'll only have to fill up with bathrobes and sweaters. For really short trips use the one-suiter. You can get one just big enough for one complete change of clothes, and some of them even have a hanger for the suit. If you think you can get along with just one suit (the one you're wearing), then your attaché case may suffice, since all you'll need will be a change of shirt, tie, socks and underwear.

For longer trips, the regular suitcase (in leather, processed fabric or synthetic) with a zipper or clasp fastening is suitable.

HOW TO FOLD A SUIT

For fold you must, if your suitcase has no hanger. One essential is to avoid overpacking or jamming clothes into the suitcase, because this pressure will only make creases. Of course, this is no problem if your suits are crease-resistant knits.

Now, step by step, here is how to fold a suit no matter what its fabric:

1. Start out by fastening the middle button of the jacket and then hold the jacket in both hands at each shoulder, shaking it gently to remove the wrinkles.

2. Next place the jacket button side down on a chest, bed or table, smoothing it out so that there is a minimum of wrinkles. If it has flaps on the pockets be sure the flaps are on the outside.

3. Fold each side of the jacket back from the shoulder to the bottom so that the edge of the sleeve at about the elbow is in line with the center seam in back of the jacket. To minimize wrinkles place a sheet of crumpled tissue paper lengthwise between the sleeves. Smooth them out carefully.

4. Fold the jacket in half and place it in the suitcase either vertically or horizontally depending on the shape of the suitcase.

5. Folding the trousers or slacks is relatively simple. After brushing, close the zipper of the trousers, fold in half and place at the bottom of the suitcase. If by any chance the waist measurement is more than average, then it's well to fold the trousers or slacks over a vertical line at the seat. If the suitcase is a small size it may be necessary to fold the trousers twice in order to reduce the overall length. The trousers or slacks should be placed at the bottom of the suitcase and the jacket above it.

SELECTING THE PROPER-SIZE LUGGAGE

Wherever you're going, and whatever the time you're going to spend, there's a suitcase somewhere that is just the right size and shape for you. It's no problem to find it; stores that carry any type of luggage usually have a wide variety.

Fabric suitcases are sophisticated-looking, and the vinyls are enormously popular because they're not only lightweight and durable, but also stain-, tear- and scuff-resistant. They can be cleaned with soap and water, and many of the vinyls now are being made to resemble suede. Not that leather is to be ignored. Far from it. Especially smart are the leather bags with markings still on them—scratches, brand marks, et cetera.

Briefly, here is the choice of styles available:

The One-Suiter

This small suitcase is most often seen with "soft" sides, zippered closure, and sometimes a detachable shoulder strap. There are water-repellent cottons with calf trim, complete with hangers and rack, that can serve as a briefcase, weekender, grooming kit and overnighter all in one. The one-suiter is small enough in overall size to rate as a "carry-on" suitcase with the airlines.

The Suit Frame

Since one-suiters are pretty low on space, if you don't take particular precautions while packing you may wrinkle your suit. Enter the suit frame. This little gimmick enables you to pack your suit neatly and make sure it doesn't get mashed into a corner in transit. Basically it consists of a square metal frame that folds in half. A hanger is attached to one side and a rod goes across the middle. You start out by folding your trousers separately and placing them in the bottom of the case (you don't need any frame for them). Then the jacket is placed on the hanger with the center rod in front and the lower rod behind. The sleeves are folded around the sides of the jacket, and then the frame is folded over itself twice. It makes quite a neat package, and it will stay that way until you unpack it many miles away.

Expanded One-Suiter

This model combines suitcase and briefcase. In the service of "economy" one could hardly ask for a more efficient use of space.

The Two-Suiter

Let us say you're going off on a longer trip. The one-suiter isn't big enough, so you'll have to use a two-suiter (and of course you'll have to check it before you board the plane). One of the tricky things about it is, again, packing the suits properly. If you aren't going to use the frame, try folding them this way:

Lay the trousers in the case. Place the jacket on top of them with the sleeves folded in front. Then fold in the bottoms of the trousers and, over them, the ends of the jacket. This makes a secure, interlocking bundle that stays put.

The Stand-up Bag

A kind of portable closet on rollers, it stands about a yard tall and resembles the canvas fold-over wardrobe bags, except that it can't be folded. A capacious item, it can be made to hold even more by using two ingenious triangular plastic packs. These fit right above each shoulder and hold small things like socks, handkerchiefs and jewelry.

HOW TO PACK

Shoes

There are several methods. One is to put all your clothes in the suitcase, then stick your shoes at the ends with the soles toward the sides of the bag. Another technique, if you're only taking one pair, is to place the shoes along the hinge end of the luggage (which becomes the bottom when standing upright). For two pairs, place the shoes sole to heel, also along the hinge end. Still another way is to put shoes in the bottom of the luggage first, and then pack everything else around them.

Hats

Stuff the crown of the hat with some of your so-called crushables (i.e., underwear), then pack more crushables around the crown and brim.

Shirts

Put each shirt in folded—as it comes folded from the laundry—in its own plastic bag. Then stack each shirt, alternating the collars so that you'll have a compact rectangular package. Keeping the shirts this way, even after you've arrived at your destination, makes it easier to get at them.

Ties

Invest in a tie case. Or make your own tie case with two pieces of cardboard (from your shirts) cut to the length of a folded-over tie; and then sandwich your ties between the pieces of cardboard. Ties can also be rolled up tight. By stretching them taut and smooth in a roll you avoid wrinkles, and the rolls can be used to fill up odd corners of your bag.

Belts

Roll them by sticking the end through the buckle and then curling the end inward. The belt will coil tight and won't jiggle loose.

PACKING A SUITCASE

Socks

Roll each pair together from toe to top, tightly.

Underwear

Fold undershirt and shorts in thirds lengthwise. Place the shorts inside the undershirt and roll them up together.

HOW TO TAKE CARE OF LEATHER GOODS

Dirt, grease, excessive moisture and humidity are the great enemies of leather. Smoke, tobacco fumes, soot, acid fumes are injurious. A leather article that's kept clean and away from excessive dampness will last much longer. Storing leather goods in closets with little air and some humidity wil cause deterioration of the leather, and may also promote the formation of mold or mildew.

Most leathers have an oil and grease content that's a valuable ingredient, since it preserves the leather. It's important, therefore, to renew periodically the oil in the leather by an application of a good grade of saddle soap especially along all edges and seams:

First clean the bag or case with a damp cloth and a lather made of a mild soap. Rub with a dry, soft-nap cloth, and while still slightly damp apply saddle soap or a light coat of neat's-foot or castor oil. Allow to dry and then remove excess soap or oil and polish with a good neutral wax.

Personal and fancy leather goods are made of such a great variety of leathers that no general instructions can be given. For calf leathers, polishing with a good neutral cream will prove beneficial. Pigskin responds to a good going over with a saddle soap and then, when dry, with a good wax polish. Morocco leathers should be polished periodically with a white or neutral shoe cream. Alligator, too, is improved by an occasional going over with a white or neutral cream polish. Leathers finished in high colors or in écrasé finishes should be left alone; attempts to clean them will generally injure their appearance.

Rawhide luggage can be cleaned with a damp cloth and soapsuds, and then dried with a clean cloth. This should remove most of the superficial dirt. For embedded stains rub a ball of steel wool over the stained areas; the abrasive action of the steel wool will erase the stain. Then apply a coat of lacquer or varnish and allow to dry. Polish with a wax emulsion.

Patent leathers will last longer if treated frequently with a light coat of castor oil to prevent cracking (or use one of the special patent spray polishes), followed by an application of a good neutral cream or wax.

Suede is difficult to clean. Spots can be removed with benzene.

A wire brush will clean superficial dirt and bring up the nap. Care should be taken not to rub hard or the surface may be damaged.

TRAVEL TIPS FOR THE CRUISE SHIP

You're skimming the briny heading toward Caribbean or Mediterranean ports of call, and you have no concern about the weight of your luggage. Still you don't want to overpack. And you do have some questions about what your luggage should include. For instance, what will you need for life aboard ship? What will you require for shore excursions?

Well, life aboard a cruise ship is basically informal, so lightweight, easy-care clothes are the rule. But that doesn't mean you should leave your formal wear hibernating at home. On the contrary. Formal attire is the thing for dinner aboard ship; just remember this cardinal rule: You do *not* dress formal on sailing day or the day before you arrive back in home port. On those two evenings a suit or sports jacket/blazer and slacks—with shirt and tie—will do just fine.

So far as formal attire aboard ship is concerned, you can be as colorful as you like. Many men still prefer the black, midnight blue or summer white dinner jacket, but if you hanker after color, don't deny yourself. As already noted in our section on Formal Evening Wear, pastels, stripes and vibrant colors are all acceptable. And while mohair and worsted are still up there among the leading warm-weather fabrics for formal wear, there are also the enormously popular double knits—the blends of, say, Dacron and wool or Dacron and rayon—and of course denim.

Shorts and swimsuits are invariably banned from the ship's dining room. You're expected to wear a jacket for all meals there, but for a buffet lunch on deck you can wear whatever you damn well please. For luncheon in the dining room, however, wear a sports jacket and sport shirt. But nobody will mind if for the conventional sports jacket you substitute a long-sleeved safari jacket or a bush coat, especially if you've added a colorful silk ascot or neckerchief to the neckline.

Still, if a sports jacket is your choice, you can go on a veritable binge of self-expression. Perhaps a buttonless white linen sprinkled all over with multicolored dots. Or an unconstructed, unpadded lightweight brushed cotton enlivened with bold checks. A floral-patterned denim. A candy-striped knitted polyester. A bright red double-knit cotton. A windowpane-checked seersucker. A rousing cotton madras. As you can see, the choice is virtually limitless.

For playtime on deck you might choose to go bare-chested, keeping a sport shirt or the jacket half of a cabana set handy for when you must move from the sun-splattered deck to indoor air-conditioning. Most men, however, play in a short-sleeved sport shirt and a pair of slacks, jeans or cutoffs. Now a word about cutoffs: you can take a pair of lightweight slacks or blue jeans and with scissors cut them off at thigh level and have yourself a pair of homemade cutoffs. Or, if you like, you can buy a ready-made pair in just about any jeans shop. Cutoffs may have that artfully ragged, scissors-cut look, or may boast neat 2-inch-wide cuffs. The main thing is that they are inches shorter than Bermuda walk shorts.

Here are a few suggestions for on-deck fun-and-games wear: a cotton tank top with knit slacks; short-sleeved madras shirt and cutoffs; cotton denim overalls—fitted, shaped and flare-bottomed—worn with or without a shirt; a cotton duck beach shirt and tartan plaid jean-style slacks. Any of these combinations would be appropriate and since you're going to be at sea for a few days at least, you could conceivably take them all along—mix and match—and emerge as the most imaginatively dressed landlubber on board.

(In the event you may be sailing out of a port where it's cool weather, pack a turtleneck sweater or, at the very least, a sleeveless sweater that will come in handy until you hit the balmier waters.)

Pack at least two pairs of swim shorts. Some lines specify that "Cruise members are requested to wear robes over their bathing suits while going to and from the pools." If a robe is mandatory on your ship, there's the tried and true terry cloth and, at the other extreme, the loose-fitting, caftan-inspired cotton robe that covers you clear down to the ankles. But whichever you choose, be certain it's a bona fide robe. A short-sleeved pullover or sailing jacket, both of which are generally considered sort of like robes for beachwear, are *not* considered robes aboard a cruise ship.

Also include in your luggage a pair of sandals to get you from your stateroom to the pool, sandals that will also go with your outfits for fun and games on deck. It's another great chance to express your individuality as you choose from a range of footwear that runs the gamut from the eminently practical rubber shower clog to the suede-laced sandal, thong sandal or boot-sandal with leather extension sole.

When dressing for shore excursions, let the port of call dictate your outfit. When in doubt, ask the social director. Sport shirt and slacks are almost always correct, but some of the resorts ashore may require a jacket and tie in their dining rooms and cocktail lounges. Your overalls and cutoffs, which are dandy for wear on deck, are off limits for onshore wear even in the most casual ports of call.

And while the suggestion of rain may sound like heresy, it does rain sometimes even on a tropical paradise. So we suggest you take along a lightweight raincoat should you happen to be on shore at one of those rare moments when the sun slips behind a cloud and an uncommonly heavy dew suddenly pours forth.

TRAVEL TIPS FOR AIR TRAVEL

The old penny-wise-pound-foolish bromide applies here. A first-class ticket for foreign travel permits you a luggage allowance of 66 pounds; a tourist/economy ticket restricts you to a luggage allowance of 44 pounds. Anything above your luggage allowance is tagged overweight and you pay for it. How much? Each additional 2.2 pounds over the free allowance is charged at one percent of the first-class one-way fare for any destination worldwide.

Since domestic air travel allows all its passengers a luggage allowance that is a little more than three times that of the 66 pounds permitted the first-class passenger for foreign travel, we'll concern ourselves here only with packing for foreign travel. So here are some suggestions on how to take along everything you'll need to look well dressed for every occasion and yet stay within the limits of your luggage allowance.

Start off by bearing in mind these basics:

A worsted suit weighs in at about 2½ pounds.
A shirt weighs about ½ pound.
A pair of shoes weighs about 4 pounds.
And why wait until you check in at the airport to discover how much your luggage weighs? Use your bathroom scale.

FIRST CLASS—SUMMER TRAVEL *

Wear a wrinkle-proof double-knit blazer suit; shirt and tie or knit sport shirt; straw hat; and black loafers which can be worn later with your dinner clothes. You might consider an all-white double-knit suit whose top *and* bottom parts can be worn for sportswear, too. And since a lightweight raincoat is a necessity, carry yours over your arm as you climb aboard.

Pack 2 pairs of slacks; 1 summer sports jacket, 2 tropical-weight suits; 1 lightweight dinner suit, formal shirt and tie, waistcoat or cummerbund, formal jewelry (unless, of course, you definitely know you won't be dressing formal, in which case you'll have space for another tropical-weight suit and a couple of extra shirts); 3 sport shirts; 2 swimsuits; 1 pair cotton canvas espadrilles or thong sandals; 2 pairs of shoes (1 sturdy pair for sightseeing); 6 dress shirts; ties; socks (1 pair over-the-calf black or midnight blue nylon for dinner suit); underwear; 2 pairs of pajamas; 1 lightweight robe that can double as a beach coat; 1 pair folding bedroom slippers in zipper case; 1 pair rubbers in zipper case; belts; suspenders (if you're taking along a dinner suit); 3 pairs of lightweight metal shoe trees; clothes brush; shaving kit (if you're taking an electric razor, include international plugs).

TOURIST/ECONOMY CLASS—SUMMER TRAVEL *

Wear the outfit already suggested for the first-class passenger, but with this one difference: substitute a darker-color knit suit for the all-white knit, since white may produce some cleaning problems

---

* We've assumed that you're planning to spend at least a weekend at some resort. If that's not on your itinerary, however, you can replace the swimsuit(s) and sport shirt(s)—as well as the espadrilles or thong sandals if you're going first class—with some extra dress shirts and accessories.

while traveling and your reduced luggage allowance doesn't permit you as much variety in your wardrobe.

Pack 2 pairs of slacks; 2 summer sports jackets (make one a solid-color blazer); 1 lightweight dinner suit, formal shirt and tie, waistcoat or cummerbund, formal jewelry (unless, of course, you definitely know you won't be dressing formal, in which case you might wish to add the all-white knit sport suit and a few extra shirts); 2 sport shirts; 1 swimsuit; 2 pairs of shoes (1 sturdy pair for sightseeing; beach shoes you can buy at any European resort); 4 dress shirts; ties; socks (1 pair over-the-calf black or midnight blue nylon for dinner suit); underwear; 2 pairs of pajamas; 1 lightweight robe that can double as a beach coat; 1 pair folding bedroom slippers in zipper case; 1 pair rubbers in zipper case; belts; suspenders (if you're taking along a dinner suit); 3 pairs of lightweight metal shoe trees; clothes brush; shaving kit (if you're taking an electric razor, include international plugs).

FIRST CLASS — WINTER TRAVEL

Wear a double-knit suit; shirt and tie; hat; gloves; black loafers that can also be worn with dinner clothes; and a waterproofed winter topcoat (preferably dark to wear over dinner clothes), which will make the addition of a raincoat unnecessary. Carry a storm coat in leather, suede or pile-lined denim for casual outerwear.

Pack 2 suits (at least one of the suits you pack should be a solid dark color), or 1 suit and a blazer and slacks; 1 turtleneck pullover; 4 dress shirts; 1 dinner suit, formal shirt and tie, waistcoat or cummerbund, formal jewelry (unless you know for certain you won't be dressing formal, in which case you'll have room for another suit and dress shirt); 2 pairs of shoes (1 sturdy pair for sightseeing); ties; socks (1 pair over-the-calf black or midnight blue nylon for formal wear); underwear; 2 pairs of pajamas; 1 wool robe; 1 pair folding bedroom slippers in zipper case; 1 pair rubbers or stretch rubber boots in zipper case; belts; suspenders (if you're taking a dinner suit); scarves; gloves; 3 pairs of lightweight metal shoe trees; clothes brush; shaving kit (include international plugs if you're taking an electric razor).

TOURIST / ECONOMY CLASS — WINTER TRAVEL

Wear the outfit laid out for the first-class passenger.

Pack 1 solid-color blazer; 2 pairs of slacks (both of which should go with the blazer and the jacket of your travel suit); 1 turtleneck sweater; 3 dress shirts; 1 dinner suit, formal shirt and tie, waistcoat or cummerbund, formal jewelry (if you have at least one formal occasion on your agenda, otherwise here's your opportunity to add another suit and dress shirt); 2 pairs of shoes (1 sturdy pair for sightseeing); ties; socks (1 pair over-the-calf black or midnight blue nylon for formal wear); underwear; 2 pairs of pajamas; 1 wool robe; 1 pair folding bedroom slippers in zipper case; 1 pair rubbers or stretch rubber boots in zipper case; belts; suspenders (if you're taking a dinner suit); scarves; gloves; 3 pairs of lightweight metal shoe trees; clothes brush; shaving kit (include international plugs if you're taking an electric razor).

CHAPTER THIRTEEN

From Jeans to Jobs

LEGEND has it that back in the early pre-Peacock sixties, a senior veep with a major blue chip corporation fixed a jaundiced eye on the tasseled loafers of a junior executive and growled: "That young fellow can't be very serious about his career."

Time marches on. And now here you are about to be graduated into the business world, where anything-with-a-pair-of-jeans doesn't hold up as a fashion rule. Still, even in the most conservative corporation, the dark suit with white shirt and conservative tie is no longer *the* uniform. In short, the peacocks are beginning to outnumber the penguins. That's not meant to suggest, however, that a jump suit is acceptable office garb, or even that you can dispense with a necktie. For if you're about to embark on a career in the business world, you must look as though *you* mean business. So you must use common sense when it comes to building your basic wardrobe. If a career in the advertising agency world is your goal, that's one thing. But if it's banking, securities or insurance— that's something else. In fact, even within the boundaries of advertising there are different sartorial looks depending upon your job status.

A former copywriter we know who is today one of the youngest big-agency presidents in the world has *two* wardrobes: his work clothes and his meet-the-client clothes. Work clothes may include a pair of bell bottom jeans, a sweater and a shirt sans tie. But for a meeting with a client or prospective client, our prexy runs around the corner to his penthouse apartment and changes into a suit and tie. "You have to dress appropriately when going to a client," he says. "To look too casual would be rude and unprofessional." But with his long hair, wide mustache and a shaped navy velvet suit, nobody is ever going to mistake him for one of his account men.

After all, would an account man wear a velvet suit? "Our clients would look askance," says our young prexy.

Over at the agency of ad man Jerry (*From Those Wonderful Folks Who Gave You Pearl Harbor*) Della Femina, this same double standard exists. His long-haired art director may wear a leather jacket and jeans one day, a shaped Cardin jacket and hopsack bell bottoms the next. "I dress the way I feel. I hardly ever wear a tie," says Mr. Art Director. "But I put one on for new business presentations. After all, older men tend to regard you more seriously when you're wearing a tie, and also there's less possibility of a hassle."

Account executives at this agency are also what you would call traditionalists. "We dress in this business by definition," one of them told us.

"The major blue chip company is basically conservative," opines one topnotch New York executive placement specialist. "And this can't help but be reflected by the people who choose to work for them."

HOW TO DRESS FOR A JOB INTERVIEW

But *you* are considering going to work for one of them, and you certainly don't intend to reflect their conservatism. How to dress? With flair. With good taste. And be cheered by this fact: as more of your breed of liberated man enter the corporate world, the sartorial picture will become brighter.

It's difficult to lay down blanket rules, since so much depends (as we've already seen in the ad agencies) on where you work and what you do there. So take a look around the premises and try to adapt without losing your individuality.

Work in the suburbs and you may never have to wear a business suit; a sports jacket, slacks and sport shirt may suffice. But work in an office in the city, and a business suit, shirt and tie are essential; still, your shirt can be boldly striped, your tie dynamic and your suit smartly shaped.

As the veep at a big city bank puts it: "We simply expect our people to be dressed in good taste. *Good taste* is the key word."

But we choose to think that the timeliest comment of all was made by a corporate personnel director who said: "I wouldn't want to hire a young man who didn't wear contemporary-looking clothes. After all, we want young people who are representative of youth today." In other words, one sure way to reach today's all-important youth market is to have young executives aboard who are aware and *look* it.

Now let's get down to specifics:

The Interview

It's putting-it-on-the-line time. You on one side of the desk and Mr. Prospective Employer on the other. Naturally, how you look is important. Surveys, in fact, have shown that while 75 percent of the communications we "receive" are verbal, only about 15 percent of the information we retain in our memories is received through our ears. The other 85 percent comes through our eyes—from the printed word or from the things we see. So when you're out to impress Mr. Prospective Employer that you mean business, *look* like a young business executive. And today you can manage it without sacrificing one whit of style. You can and should dress with a sense of vitality.

For example, for your interview you might wear a solid-color blazer suit, or a blazer jacket with solid-color or patterned slacks. Either way, you're comfortable and contemporary. Add a solid-color shirt and foulard tie . . . or a striped shirt and a checked or plaid tie. A silk pocket handkerchief. A pair of slip-ons or demi-boots. Over-the-calf socks. *You look great!*

An outfit like that should be acceptable anywhere in today's business world, but should you come across a pocket of ultra-conservatism where it's frowned upon as too casual, it's unlikely you'd want to work there anyway. For if they're that antique in their attitude toward a man's garb, you can be fairly certain their business practices could use some updating, too.

The main thing to bear in mind is that your clothes should express you but never distract from you. It's like when you give a speech. What you wear should express you, be pleasing to the eye, but must never get between you and your audience. You want them to listen to what you say, not concentrate on what you wear. And the same principle applies to a job interview. You are selling *you,* not your wardrobe. But never forget that what you wear is one mighty potent way to create a positive impression.

A BASIC BUSINESS WARDROBE

Assuming that you're working behind a desk rather than at a lathe, we've collected for you the following wardrobe which fairly shouts executive status:

Suits

4 winter- or mid-weight suits. Consider a navy double-knit blazer suit; a camel-color corduroy; a gray windowpane plaid; and a clay- or green-toned gabardine. Or perhaps this quartet: a navy chalk-stripe worsted; a salt-and-pepper tweed; a brown flannel; and a geometric-pattern double knit in any color. *Optional:* a navy or dark brown velvet suit. The velvet suit is acceptable in some business environs, but still too avant-garde for others. Only you can decide what its impact would be at your business address.

3 summer-weight suits. Perhaps a subtly spectacular all-white or pastel-color suit of a polyester and linen blend; a miniature-checked beige or tan seersucker; a denim-color double knit. Others heartily recommended: a plaid seersucker; a beige summer corduroy; a work-shirt-blue cotton chambray.

1 lightweight blazer.

2 pairs of slacks, one solid-color and the other patterned.

Shirts

12 dress shirts—a minimum. The more, the better. At least three should be solid colors (one white will suffice). The remainder should include stripes—from skinny stripes to bold pirate stripes—and the rest a sprinkling of checks, plaids and geometric patterns. *Optional:* A plaid or striped knit body shirt with white collar and barrel cuffs.

Ties

12—a minimum. Again, the more, the better. In your collection be sure to have one rich wool challis, a brocaded tapestry, a knit, a couple of reps, one polka dot, at least one solid, a geometric, a plaid or check. *Optional:* A bow tie in a width most flattering to your facial structure.

Shoes

3 dress pairs. 2 blacks and 1 brown or vice versa. Suggestion: One pair might be a black patent leather or calf slip-on that will double for formal wear.

1 pair demiboots.

2 frankly summer pairs. Make your choice from among such luxurious-looking and keenly contemporary styles as, say, a white patent leather moccasin-style slip-on or demiboot; an oxford of natural linen and patent leather, or some other natty combination.

Outercoats

1 really sumptuous overcoat. A dark blue British warm of immensely durable cavalry twill, while not a formal coat, is dressy enough to get by with a dinner jacket for those dress-up evenings. Or you might want to consider the classic camel's hair in one of its updated versions: a wraparound or a deep-pocketed model with a collar of some young-spirited, budget-minded fur like raccoon. *Optional:* A fur coat, genuine or in a look-like-fur synthetic fiber. Perhaps a flat fur like lustrous brown bull, or a synthetic of black Orlon that resembles black seal to such a remarkable degree that it would take a seal to tell the difference. Happily, both coats are much less expensive than they look.

1 leather coat. Black or antique brown, in a soft, supple, double-breasted trench coat style. (How about one with brass buttons?)

1 topcoat or all-weather coat. Working on the premise that a topcoat has a short season in many parts of the U.S. and that therefore you owe it to yourself to look as dandy as possible those relatively few weeks a year, we suggest a calf-length coat of suede designed with the safari suit or trench coat in mind, or a shaped maxi topcoat of a tapestry wool weave. Neither of these coats, however, is exactly budget-priced, so if they're beyond you at the moment, then by all means consider a snappy-looking all-weather coat of warp knit with an interlining and a special finish that guards against rain and stain. A coat like that in dark brown or navy is so practical that buying it is almost like putting your money into government bonds.

Hats

1 soft "slouch."
1 broad-brimmed velour.
1 summer straw (at the very least), with an extroverted band, be it of perforated leather, multicolor silk stripings, an Aztec design or snakeskin. *Optional:* A fur hat, genuine or fake. High on the preferred list should be a cossack-style Persian lamb.

Raincoats

1 classic calf-length trench or safari-style coat, with a colorful detachable lining.
1 short, sporty coat. A poplin cap would be a jaunty touch with this coat.
Optional: A high-fashion patterned raincoat. Perhaps a geometric knit with a cape-type back and pockets deep enough to dive into. Or a double-breasted black-and-white herringbone-print cotton.
Rainy-day fashions certainly aren't the place to start skimping. Your impeccable garb on a rainy day when the office penguins are sloshing in wearing their what-the-hell-it's-raining outfits will earn you extra points with the upper-level executives who notice such things.

In our suit recommendations, we've taken special care to offer you (1) a variety of color that will permit you any number of sharp-minded shirt and tie combinations, and (2) fabrics that have the kind of versatility that, if the jackets are cut with sufficient flair, qualifies them to be worn weekends as sports jackets, while their trousers can double as odd pants.

The navy double-knit blazer suit jacket, for example, will look handsome paired with the trousers of the corduroy, windowpane plaid and gabardine suits. That's because it is frankly a blazer suit, which means the jacket was designed to be sporty enough for wearing as a sports jacket, too. But it would be possible for all three of the other suits in your wardrobe to be similarly designed without being identified as blazer suits. So when you go shopping for a business suit, it would be wise to go garbed in sports jacket and slacks and test out the new suit jacket's potential for sportswear there in the store before a full-length mirror.

It should go without saying that the jacket and trousers of the salt-and-pepper tweed suit can go their separate ways for sportswear. And if you were to choose a brown flannel suit that happened to have brass buttons, you would have yourself a stunning blazer sports jacket. Invest in the velvet suit and you'd really stretch your wardrobe. You'd have the makings of a super country suit with only the substitution of a turtleneck pullover in place of shirt and tie; the pants would look sensational with the jacket of your navy blazer suit; and the velvet jacket would showcase any number of slacks. The point we're trying to make must be fairly obvious by now: It's smart to invest in a suit that, by virtue of color, fabric and styling, will mix and match with the other suits in your wardrobe. The result of such canny planning will be that a stylish though economy-minded wardrobe will appear to be infinitely more affluent.

One last note: Although this wardrobe has been earmarked for the young man just starting out on his business career, it is sophisticated enough to do justice to the more mature man as well. So whether you're twenty-two or forty-two, wear it—as they say in some circles—in good health.

CHAPTER FOURTEEN

How to Remove
Spots and Stains

SHAKESPEARE'S Lady Macbeth had the right idea when she cursed, "Out, damned spot!" But the lady clearly couldn't tell a spot from a stain, for blood—her problem—is definitely a stain. And there is, you see, a difference. For one thing, a spot is easier to get rid of. So no wonder Lady M. became so unstrung.

Briefly the difference is this: a spot is a mark caused by food or liquid that has surrounded the fibers of the fabric; a stain, on the other hand, is a foreign substance that has actually worked its way into the fiber of the fabric and consequently is more tenacious. If it's a spot you're concerned with, daubing is always the first thing to do. There are some nonliquid spot removers on the market that are effective and do not leave a telltale ring. But if you're going to use a cleaning fluid, wait until the spot is dry before using it.

Removing a stain, however, calls for a bit more expertise. After all, there are greasy stains, nongreasy stains and stains that are a combination of both greasy and nongreasy substances. And no matter what its origin, *any* stain is easier to remove if you get at it while it's still fresh. The longer you wait, the tougher—or more impossible—it will be to remove it.

Basically, here are the ways you handle most stains that fall into the three categories greasy, nongreasy and combination stains:

GREASY STAINS

If the article is *washable,* you'll find regular washing (hand or machine) will remove some greasy stains. Others can be removed by rubbing soap or detergent into the stain, followed by a warm water rinsing. But on certain wash-and-wear or perm-

194

anent-press fabrics you may have to rub soap or detergent into the stain and let it stand for several hours—perhaps even overnight—before rinsing. If the stain is especially stubborn, you will need to use a special grease solvent like those used by dry cleaners, which are available at drug and grocery stores. (Many of these are mixtures of two or more grease solvents and can be either flammable or nonflammable. Naturally you are urged to read the label carefully and follow all the precautions listed by the manufacturer.)

When using a grease solvent, start by sponging the stain thoroughly with the solvent. Dry. Then repeat if necessary, since it often takes an extra application to remove a grease stain from a fabric with a special finish. A yellow stain may be left after the solvent treatment if the stain has been set by age or heat. To remove such a stain us a peroxy bleach.

If the article is *nonwashable,* start right out by sponging the stain with grease solvent. Dry. Then repeat if necessary. Should a yellow stain be left, use a peroxy bleach.

Some of the most common greasy stains are butter and margarine, car grease, furniture polish, ink (mimeograph and printing), oil (machine oil, mineral oil, fish liver oil, linseed oil, vegetable oil).

NONGREASY STAINS

If the article is *washable,* some nongreasy stains are removed by regular laundry methods; others are set by them. You may play it safe by sponging the stain with cool water or soaking it in cool water for thirty minutes or longer. Some nongreasy stains may require overnight soaking.

If the stain is especially stubborn and remains after sponging or soaking, rub soap or detergent into it and then rinse well. If the stain still remains after rinsing, use a peroxy bleach.

If the article is *nonwashable,* sponge the stain with cool water. If the stain remains, rub on soap or detergent and work it into the fabric. Rinse.

A final sponging with alcohol helps to remove the soap or detergent, as well as drying the fabric more quickly. (To make sure alcohol does not affect the dye, test alcohol on fabric first. Before sponging an acetate with alcohol, dilute the alcohol with two parts of water.)

If the stain remains after rinsing, use a peroxy bleach.

Some of the most common nongreasy stains are alcoholic beverages, catsup, chili sauce, cocoa, coffee or tea without cream, egg, fruit and fruit juices, ink (writing), milk, soft drinks, vegetable.

COMBINATION STAINS

If the article is *washable,* sponge stain with cool water or soak in cool water for thirty minutes or longer.

If the stain remains, rub soap or detergent into it and rinse well. If a greasy stain remains, sponge with a grease solvent. Repeat if necessary after the article has dried. If a colored stain remains after the fabric dries, use a peroxy bleach.

If the article is *nonwashable,* sponge stain with cool water.

If stain persists, rub on soap or detergent and work it into fabric. Rinse spot well with water and allow article to dry. If a greasy stain remains, sponge with a grease solvent. Repeat if necessary after the article has dried. If a colored stain remains after the fabric dries, use a peroxy bleach.

Some of the most common combination stains are chocolate and chocolate candy, coffee and tea with cream, gravy and meat juice, ice cream, mayonnaise and salad dressing, soups and sauces.

Of course, there are stains that require special treatment:

Antiperspirants and Deodorants

Wash or sponge stain thoroughly with soap or detergent and warm water. Rinse. If stain still remains, use a peroxy bleach.

Blood

This is a nongreasy stain and you can treat it as such but with one variation. If the stain is not removed by soap or detergent, put a few drops of ammonia on the stain and repeat treatment with detergent. Rinse. Follow with peroxy bleach treatment if necessary.

Carbon Paper

(Regular) Work soap or detergent into stain; rinse. If stain is not removed, put a few drops of ammonia on the stain and repeat treatment; rinse well. Repeat if necessary.

Cosmetics

(This means lipstick, powder, rouge, pancake makeup, liquid makeup, mascara and eye shadow.) If the article is *washable,* apply undiluted liquid detergent directly to stain or dampen stain and rub in soap or detergent until thick suds are formed. Work in until outline of stain disappears; rinse well. Repeat if necessary. (It may help to dry fabric between treatments.) If the article is *nonwashable*, sponge with a grease solvent for as long as any color is removed. If the stain remains, use method given for washable articles.

And by the way, crayon stains are removed the same way as cosmetic stains.

Grass

If the article is *washable*, work soap or detergent into stain; rinse. Or, if the fabric's dye is safe when alcohol is applied, sponge stain with alcohol. (Dilute alcohol with two parts of water for use on acetate.) If stain remains, use a peroxy bleach. If the article is *nonwashable*, use same methods as for washable articles, but try alcohol first if it's safe for dye.

Iodine

If the article is *washable*, there are actually three methods. So if one doesn't work, try another . . . and another.

1. Soak article in cool water until stain is removed; some stains require overnight soaking. If stain stays, rub it with soap or

detergent and wash in warm suds. If stain still persists, soak fabric in a solution containing 1 tablespoon of sodium thiosulfate to each pint of warm water or sprinkle the crystals on the dampened stain. Rinse well as soon as the stain is removed.

2. Moisten stain with water; then hold it in the steam from a boiling teakettle.

3. If alcohol is safe for the fabric's dye, cover the stain with a pad of cotton soaked in alcohol. (It may be necessary to keep the pad wet for several hours.) And yes, if it's an acetate fabric you're treating, dilute the alcohol with two parts of water.

If the article is *nonwashable*, try methods 2 and 3 noted above. But if steam and/or alcohol are not safe for fiber or dye or if the stain is still there after using them, cover the stain with a pad of cotton dampened in a solution of sodium thiosulfate (1 tablespoon of sodium thiosulfate to each pint of water) for about fifteen minutes. Rinse well. Repeat if necessary.

Mildew

If the article is *washable*, wash it thoroughly and then dry in sun. If stain persists, treat it with a peroxy bleach. You're urged to treat all mildew spots while they're still fresh and before the mold growth has a chance to weaken the fabric. And if the article is *nonwashable*, send it off to your favorite dry cleaner posthaste.

Paint and Varnish

There are many different kinds of paints and varnishes, and no one method will remove all stains. Read the label on the container and if a certain solvent is recommended as a thinner, you'll probably find that it will be the most effective.

If the article is *washable*, and the stain is still fresh, rub soap or detergent into the stain and wash. If stain has dried or is only partially removed by washing, then sponge with turpentine until no more paint or varnish is removed. For aluminum paint stains, trichloroethylene may be more effective than turpentine. (This solvent is not for use on Arnel or Kodel.)

While the stain is still wet with the solvent, work soap or detergent into it, put the article in hot water and soak it overnight. Thorough washing will then remove most types of paint stains. If stain remains, repeat the treatment.

If the article is *nonwashable,* and the stain is still fresh, sponge it with turpentine until no more paint is removed. For aluminum paint stains, trichloroethylene is often a more effective stain remover than turpentine, but don't use it on Arnel or Kodel.

If necessary, loosen paint by covering the stain for thirty minutes or longer with a pad of cotton dampened with the solvent. Repeat sponging.

If stain is still there, put a drop of liquid detergent on the stain and work it into the fabric with the edge of the bowl of a spoon.

Alternately, sponge the stain with turpentine and treat with detergent as many times as necessary.

If alcohol is safe for dye, sponge stain with alcohol to remove turpentine and detergent. If you're working with an acetate, dilute alcohol with two parts of water. If alcohol is unsafe for dye, sponge stain first with warm soap or detergent solution, then with water.

Perspiration

Wash or sponge the stain thoroughly with soap or detergent and warm water. (Thoroughly does not mean roughly; work carefully because some fabrics are actually weakened by perspiration— silk in particular.)

If you find that perspiration has changed the color of the fabric, try restoring it by treating with ammonia or vinegar. Apply ammonia to fresh stains; rinse. Apply vinegar to old stains; rinse.

If an oily stain remains, follow directions for greasy stains.

Remove any yellow discoloration with a peroxy bleach.

Shoe Polish

Like paint and varnish, shoe polish comes in so many variations, no one method will remove all stains. So if one of the following doesn't work, try another . . . and another.

1. Follow our directions for removing cosmetics stains.

2. Sponge stain with alcohol—assuming it's safe for the fabric's dye. And if you're working with an acetate, dilute the alcohol with two parts of water.

3. Sponge stain with grease solvent or turpentine. If you use turpentine, remove it by sponging with a warm soap or detergent solution or with alcohol.

If all else fails, try using a peroxy bleach.

Glossary

ACELE: Brand of rayon by Du Pont.

ACETATE RAYON: Rayon filaments by compound of coagulated cellulose and acetic acid.

ACID DYE: Type of dye used on animal fibers; low in holding color if fabric is washed.

ACRILAN: A synthetic fiber, extremely lightweight, noncellulosic, used in blends with cotton or wool fibers. Chemstrand's acrylic fiber.

ACRYLIC: Descriptive of fiber derived from gas and air—pertaining to an unsaturated acid obtained from acrolein by oxidation.

ADMIRALTY CLOTH: Synonym for melton cloth used for navy uniforms.

AIR CONDITIONING: Chemical process sealing short fibers into yarn.

AIRPLANE CLOTH: Sturdy cotton fabric, square-woven from combed, ply yarns for balanced strength; shirtings, sportswear.

ALLIGATOR: Skin of water reptile with square, boxlike markings; standard leather goods.

ALPACA: Close-textured fabric from long hair of alpaca. Originally cotton cloth with alpaca filling, now woven alone or with wool, mohair, rayon or cotton. Used in suits, coats, sportswear; in pile form for lining and knitted into sweaters.

ALPARGATA: Sandal or rope or hemp, features woven sole shaped to footprint, to which straps attach.

ANGOLA YARN: Spun on woolen principle. Made of 80 percent wool and 20 percent cotton. Available in overcoating of low-textured twill weave.

ANGORA: Fiber from Angora goat manufactured in combination with other fibers into mohair.

ANILINE DYE: Generally applied to any synthetic organic dye.

ANTELOPE: From skin of antelope; fine, soft, velvety texture, generally suede-finished; shoes, belts, leather goods.

APRON: Wide end of necktie.

ARALAC: A synthetic fiber derived from casein in milk.

ARGYLE: Multicolored diamond pattern, usually in wool; originally knitted in England on hand frames, now made in America on machines; socks, sweaters, ties.

ARGYLL: A tartan representing a Scottish clan.

ARMSCYE: Lower part of armhole to which sleeve is attached on coat or jacket.

ARNEL: Trademark of triacetic fiber made by Celanese Corporation of America. Used in wash-and-wear fabrics.

ASCOT: Double-knot tie with ends folded over and held in place with stickpin; formal day wear. Also, a throw-over for sportswear.

ASTRAKHAN CLOTH: A term sometimes applied to a heavy, deeppile fabric with curled loops that resemble caracul. Real astrakhan is a grade of caracul lambskin.

AVISCO: Trademark of fibers made by American Viscose Division of FMC Corporation.

AVRIL: Name of modulus rayon fiber, made by American Viscose Division of FMC Corporation.

AWNING STRIPE: Broad stripe in sturdy fabrics for awnings; also description of bold stripes for sport shirts or jackets.

BACKED CLOTH: Fabric with extra weft, or warp, woven or knitted on the back to increase thickness and weight, and achieve different color effects.

BAKU: Fine, lightweight, dull-finished fiber of buri palm from Ceylon, Malabar; straw hats.

BALBRIGGAN: Lightweight unbleached knitted yarn or cotton, wool or rayon for socks, underwear, sweaters, pajamas.

BAL COLLAR: Collar of a Balmacaan coat; a high military collar that may be worn turned up and buttoned or lying flat. The collar is a band of material approximately 3½ inches wide.

BAL FASTENING: The best-known fastening in men's shoes, it has a V construction that starts at the top of the vamp and features a series of eyelets through which the shoelaces are threaded.

BALIBUNTAL: Fine, lightweight, glossy straw fibers imported from Thailand for hat; also balibuntl.

BALLOON CLOTH: Fine, closely woven, plain-weave cotton similar to airplane cloth but of finer weave; used for shirtings, sportswear.

BALLOON TOE: High, full-rounded shoe tip.

BALMACAAN: Loose-fitting topcoat or overcoat with short, military collar, raglan sleeves, front closure buttoning under collar.

BALMORAL (castle): Laced shoe with closed "throat"; abbreviation bal used: bal shoe.

BAND: Strip of fabric on hat or other article.

BANDANNA: Bright-colored square of cotton, silk; used as handkerchief, scarf.

BANDOLIER CLOTH: Strong, coarse-weave fabrics used for military cartridge belts; types applicable for civilian sport belts.

BANGKOK: Thin, smooth fiber used in open-weave straw hats.

BANNOCKBURN: A type of all-wool tweed suiting made of double-twist yarns.

BARATHEA: (1) Pebble-weave fabric in silk, rayon or cotton combination; for neckwear, cummerbunds, trim on evening wear. (2) Same fabric in worsted used for evening clothes.

BAREFACE FABRIC: Term generally applied to any cloth or fabric entirely without nap.

BARK CLOTH: Cloth made by beating inner tree bark; tapa cloth.

BARLEYCORN: Small pattern of tweed or woolen, achieved by weave.

BARREL CUFF: Single attached shirt cuff on shirt, unstarched, with buttonhole closure.

BAR-SHAPED TIE: Narrow four-in-hand necktie, with apron of even width.

BASIC DYE: Used on wool, silk and mordanted cotton; poor color resistance.

BASKET WEAVE: Plain fabric with warp and filling threads woven together to produce plaited effect; shirtings, sportswear.

BASQUE BERET: Round-crown, close-fitting cap with no visor or brim, as worn in Basque country.

BATIK: Originally process in which parts of fabric are coated with wax and only uncovered area takes dye; now imitated in machine printing.

BATISTE: Sheer cotton or spun-rayon fabric woven of combed yarns, with mercerized finish on cotton; for shirts, shorts.

BATTING: Carded cotton or wool in sheets and rolls, used for outerwear interlining and padding.

BATTLE JACKET: Waist-length, fly-front, single-breasted jacket used by Army, World War II; adapted to sportswear.

BATWING: Synonym for butterfly bow tie.

BEAU BRUMMELL: Famous dandy and friend of Prince of Wales, later George IV; Brummell also a brand of men's neckwear.

BEAVER: Fur fiber, shiny, smooth, silklike texture; used extensively in felt hat manufacture.

BEAVER CLOTH: Heavy, double-woven, smooth-faced woolen overcoating; soft, very long nap.

BEDFORD CORD: Strong, rib-weave fabric with raised lengthwise cords running in warp direction; in all-wool, silk, cotton, rayon or combination fibers; mostly sport clothing.

BEEFEATER'S HAT: Type of headpiece worn by British Yeomen of the Guard.

BEER JACKET: White denim work jacket, traditionally worn by Princeton seniors in spring.

BELLOWS PLEAT: Pocket with folds or pleats on three sides for expansion.

BELLOWS TONGUE: Broad folding tongue stitched to shoe quarter on either side to prevent water penetration; sport, work shoes.

BELT: Leather strap or band of fabric with buckle or fastener for wear at waist.

BEMBERG: Filament rayon of the cuprammonium type, made by Beaunit Corporation.

BENCH-MADE: Shoes strictly handmade by one craftsman; used for shoes featuring hand-sewn soles.

BENGALINE: Heavier-than-faille fabric featuring fine weave and filling cords. In silk, wool, rayon warp with softly spun worsted or cotton filling. Used as trim for men's evening wear, robes.

BENGAL STRIPES: Boldly colored stripes of fabric originally exported from Bengal, India; primarily for sport shirts, pajamas or beachwear.

BERET: Brimless, unvisored, tam-effect cap of felt or fabric.

BESOM: Type of pocket with stitched fold on upper and lower edges.

BIRD'S-EYE: Small geometrical pattern with a dot, suggestive of a bird's eye; used in fabrics for men's suits and neckwear.

BLADE: Extra fullness at jacket shoulder blade; originally designed by English tailors.

BLAZER: A sports jacket in a blazer fabric (principally flannel, linen, denim, cotton, double knit, velvet) whose trim distinguishes it from the usual sports jacket.

BLAZER SUIT: Any suit in a blazer fabric whose jacket is sporty enough to also be worn as a blazer sports jacket.

BLEACHING: Process for removal of impurities in fabrics by exposure to sun or chemical action to obtain clear whites for even dyeing, printing.

BLEND: Term used to describe yarn obtained when two or more fibers are combined in spinning process.

BLIND STITCH: Concealed stitch.

BLOCK PATTERN: Large square design; may be woven or printed.

BLOCK PRINTING: Hand process of printing fabrics with design carved on wooden blocks.

BLUCHER: Open-throat laced shoe.

BODY (of fabric): Solid compact or firm feel of fabric. Used in testing, determining quality.

BODY SUIT: One-piece underwear usually of woven nylon, with short sleeves, no legs and, sometimes, a button front and long fashion collar allowing it to double as a form-fitting sport shirt.

BOOK LINEN: Firm, sized linen, used as stiffening for collars and belts.

BOOT: Any footwear that extends higher than the top of the ankle.

BOTTLE GREEN: Dark green color similar to shade of glass bottles.

BOUCLÉ YARN: Wool, rayon, silk, linen, cotton, polyester or acrylic yarn with loops that give fabric rough appearance.

BOUTONNIERE: Flower or cluster of flowers worn in left lapel of jacket; may be natural or artificial.

BOWLER: Stiff-brimmed, hard, rounded-crown hat (synonym for derby); black, gray, brown.

BOW TIE: Type of necktie tied with two looped ends and two straight ends.

BOX COAT: Loose fitting topcoat, overcoat, jacket, with set-in sleeve, usually single-breasted, button-through or fly front.

BOXFORD COLLAR: Widespread, button-down shirt collar with stitching set back well from edge.

BOX PLEAT: Pleat with edges folded in opposite directions; used on jackets and shirts.

BRACES: English term for suspenders.

BRADFORD SPINNING: English method of spinning wool into worsted yarn. The wool is thoroughly oiled before it is combed, producing a smooth, lustrous yarn.

BRAID: Narrow ribbon or fabric strip used for trimming, binding or other ornamentation. Used on side seams of dress trousers; also robes, hats.

BRIEFS: A knitted short with pouch front, no legs and elasticized waistband.

BRILLIANTINE: Plain- or twill-weave fabric; cotton warp, worsted or mohair filling; linings.

BRIMS-UP: Soft felt or straw hat with medium brim turned up all around.

BRITISH WARM: Short, double-breasted topcoat, overcoat, flared from waist to bottom, usually of fleece fabric; originally military.

BROADCLOTH: Tight, plain-woven, lustrous cotton or rayon cloth with crosswise rib, for shirts, sportswear. Also identified with smooth woolen fabric with napped face and twill back.

BROCADE: Rich jacquard-woven fabric with allover interwoven design of raised figures or flowers. From French word meaning "to ornament."

BROGUE: Heavy oxford shoe with large perforated design, usually wing-tip.

BROLLY: British term for umbrella.

BRUSHING: Finishing process in which circular brushes raise nap on knitted or woven fabric.

BUCKET HOOD: As seen on the duffel coat, it hangs in back like a pouch. Some, however, are attached to the coat via buttons or zipper and can be detached.

BUCKLE: Closure consisting of frame and usually a single tooth. Ring buckle consists of two rings on one end through which the other end slips and holds firmly.

BUCKRAM: Stiff-finish cotton fabric for interlining garments, shoes, leather goods.

BUCKSKIN: Velvet-finish leather derived from deer and elk, buffed; gloves, shoes, etc.

BUFFALO CHECK: Block or square design of fabric, often red and black.

BUFFALO LEATHER: From domesticated land and water buffalo; rough grain, substitute for cattle hides in shoes, luggage leathers.

BUNTING: Closely woven wool or cotton; primarily used for flags and decorations, and also for sport shirts.

BURGUNDY: Dark red similar to color of Burgundy wine.

BURI: Fiber from fronds of talipot palm, grown in Philippines and used for straw or fiber hats.

BURNISH: To shine metal by rubbing and also descriptive of colors that have a polished look.

BUSHELING: Clothing alternation.

BUSH JACKET: Single-breasted, belted, shirt type of jacket with four pockets.

BUTCHER LINEN: Plain, woven crash fabric for sportswear.

BUTTERFLY TIE: Necktie cut with flared ends, narrow knot and neckband.

BUTTON-DOWN COLLAR: Shirt-collar points fastened to shirt with buttons and buttonholes.

BUTTON GLOVE: Short-length glove with button closure at wrist.

BUTTON-THROUGH: Closure on jacket or coat with buttonholes cut through entire nap of fabric.

CABANA: Small beach house; also casual clothes for wear at beach: set of shirt or coat and shorts.

CABLE STITCH: Overlapping knit stitch, machine or hand, simulating cable; socks, sweaters.

CABRETTA LEATHER: From Brazilian sheepskin; smooth, tight-grained; gloves, shoes, outerwear.

CADET: Refers to short-fingered gloves.

CALENDERING: Finishing process, mechanical; gives hard, smooth, glossy, embossed designs to cloth.

CALFSKIN: Skin of calf, soft, durable; gloves, shoes, all leather goods.

CALICO: An old term for a plain-woven printed cotton cloth.

CAMBRIC: Closely woven cotton fabric calendered on right side with slight gloss, usually white; shirts, underwear, handkerchiefs; originally linen.

CAMEL'S HAIR: Soft, wool-like texture, varies from light tan to brownish black. Used alone or combined with wool; coats, suits, sweaters, sportswear.

CANVAS: Cotton or linen fabric with an even, heavy weave.

CAP: Fabric head covering with tam top of one- or eight-piece construction with visor.

CAPESKIN: Tight, close-grain leather from haired sheep; gloves, leather goods.

CAPROLAN: Trade name of nylon fiber manufactured by Allied Chemical Corporation.

CARDIGAN: Collarless sweater or jacket with or without sleeves, button-through.

CARDING: Manufacturing term for machine blending and mixing of wool stocks to prepare for spinning. Removes impurities, separates fibers into continuous, untwisted strands.

CARPINCHO: Skin obtained from water rodent, similar to pigskin; elastic, soft; fine gloves, leather goods.

CARROTING: Brushing process applied to furs, utilizing solution of mercury and nitric acid. Enables matting or felting of fibers in subsequent operations. Term particularly applied to hat-making.

CASEIN: Fiber produced from skim milk, resembles wool. Blended with wool, mohair, cotton or rayon to weave or knit into fabric used in clothing. Combined with rabbit hair for felt hat bodies. Used without blending for interlining.

CASHMERE: Fabric made of hair of Cashmere goats from the Himalaya region of India, in twill and herringbone weaves; soft finish; used in all types of men's clothing, sportswear.

CASSIMERE: Woolen suiting in twill weave which shows prominently due to clear finish.

CASTOR BEAVER: Heavy-milled, face-finished, all-wool cloth, lighter in weight than ordinary beaver; used for overcoats.

CAVALRY TWILL: Sturdy-weave fabric with pronounced raised diagonal cord of wool, cotton, spun rayon, worsted; military uniforms, sportswear. Synonym for tricotine.

CELANESE: Trademark for textile and other products of Celanese Corporation.

CELLULOSE: Vegetable substance, refined; natural fiber used in rayon manufacture.

CHALLIS: Lightweight, fine-spun, closely woven worsted fabric in spun rayon or spun rayon and wool blends; may be dyed or printed; neckwear, pajamas.

CHAMBRAY: Fabric woven with colored warp and white filling, giving mottled colored surface, in cotton or spun rayon with small plain-weave effect; shirts, sportswear, pajamas.

CHAMOIS: Sheep or lambskin with grain removed; velvet finish, supple, porous; creamy yellow color; gloves, linings.

CHAMOIS CLOTH: Napped, sheared and dyed cotton fabric simulating chamois leather; gloves, sportswear.

CHARVET: Reverse rep fabric with double-ridge effect. Originally called Regence, but name is now associated with firm of Charvet et Fils; neckwear, handkerchiefs, mufflers.

CHESTERFIELD: Beltless, semifitted, single- or double-breasted overcoat for town wear; may have velvet collar.

CHEVIOT: Coarse, rough-napped fabric, originally made of Cheviot sheep wool. Now made of curly worsted, woolen yarns or spun rayon and wool blends. In twill and herringbone weaves; suits, topcoats, sportswear.

CHEVRON WEAVE: Broken-twill weave with zigzag effect produced by alternating direction of the twill; similar to herringbone; suits, topcoats.

CHINCHILLA CLOTH: Twill-weave fabric, either pure wool or cotton and wool, with napped surface of tufts or nubs. Double-faced with woven plaid or knitted back; outer coats.

CHINO CLOTH: Term used to designate a particular type of all-cotton twill, used in military uniforms; also fabric for slacks, blend of polyester and cotton.

CHLORINATED WOOL: Chemically treated woolens to decrease shrinkage and increase acceptability to dye.

CHUKKA: Ankle-high boot with two eyelets; suede or smooth leather, rubber or leather soles.

CIRCULAR KNIT: Hand- or machine-knit stitch, producing tubular fabric for socks, underwear, sportswear, neckwear.

CLEAR-FACE OR FINISHED WORSTED: Fabric of tightly twisted worsted yarns; closely sheared and scoured to show weave; smooth surface; suitings.

CLOCKS: Embroidered or other vertical design decorating each side of sock.

CLUB BOW TIE: Straight-cut tie for evening wear, generous center knot; white when worn with tailcoat, black or midnight blue with dinner jacket.

COCONUT STRAW: Palm-frond fiber plaited into braid effect for straw hats.

COLLAR (shoe): Narrow leather strip stitched around top of shoe for ornamental effect.

COLLAR-ATTACHED SHIRT: Standard shirt with fused, soft or standard collar attached to neckband.

COLLAR RISE: Height of neckband at back on collar-attached shirt.

COLLAR STAND: Height of neckband at front on collar-attached shirt.

COLOR COORDINATION: (1) Merchandising and promotion of harmonizing colors in different departments carrying merchandise for entire ensemble. (2) Fashion effect.

COMBING: Process which produces even, compact, finer, smoother yarn by eliminating shorter fibers and arranging yarn in parallel lines. Advanced form of carding.

COMMAND COLLAR: Widespread attached shirt collar with stitching half-inch from edge.

CONCEALED HOOD: As the name implies, it is concealed within the collar of the coat or jacket and is held in place by buttons or a zipper.

CONTINUOUS FILAMENT: Synthetic and regenerated fibers manufactured in continuous form—as distinguished from all natural fibers except silk.

CONVERTIBLE COLLAR: One which may be worn up or down, fastened or open.

CORD: (1) Rib-surface fabric. (2) Product formed by twisting two or more ply yarns together.

CORDOVAN: Leather from shell of horse butts; nonporous, long-wearing, with waxy finish; shoes, leather accessories.

CORDUROY: Cotton, rayon, cut-pile fabric woven with wide or narrow wale formed by using extra filling; foundation of either plain or twill weave; sportswear, boys' wear.

CORKSCREW: Worsted suiting of twisted yarns woven spirally, concealing inside filling; clear finish; prominent weave; herringbones, twills, stripes.

COTTON: Soft fiber from seed pod of cotton plant. Spun into yarn and thread for knitting, weaving; bulk of world crop is from U.S.A.

COUNT: In yarn, size or weight. In cloth, number of warp and weft yarns per inch in woven cloth.

COUNTER: Stiffening at heel to keep back of shoe in shape.

COVERT: Woolen fabric closely woven with two yarns of different colors in warp and single color in filling giving mottled appearance; twill weave, in solid colors or patterns; topcoats, sportswear, suits; available in spun rayon, spun rayon and wool or cotton.

CRASH: Coarse fabric with rough, irregular surface obtained by weaving thick, uneven cotton, linen or spun-rayon yarns. Smoother-weave woolen used for men's suiting, sportswear.

CRAVENETTE: Trade name for water-repelling treatment applied to textile fabrics and garments.

CRENELATED DESIGN: An indented pattern, resembling the outline of battlements of a fortress.

CREPE: Crinkly-surfaced fabric of silk, rayon or blends. Alternate right- and left-hand twisted yarns are used in filling; neckwear, robes.

CREPE RUBBER: Natural or synthetic rubber used in crinkled sheets; soles and heels for sport, semisport shoes.

CRESLAN: Trade name for synthetic fabric made by American Cyanamid Company.

CRESS-FACED: Term sometimes applied to woolen fabric having slight nap.

CREW NECK: Collarless opening which follows contour of neck on beach, Basque or pullover shirts, sweaters, underwear.

CRIMP: (1) Natural waviness found in wool fiber, caused by compactness of weave. More crimp denotes finer wool quality. (2) Similar waviness applied to synthetic fiber by machine.

CRINOLINE: Stiff fabric used as foundation to support edge of hems and as interlining.

CROCHET: Knitted fabric, formerly handmade with crochet hooks; now duplicated by machine with hooked needles. From the French word meaning "to hook"; neckwear, sweaters, sportswear.

CROCKING: Tendency of excess dye to rub off, particularly in napped and pile fabrics. Traceable to imperfect dyeing or inadaptability of dyestuff.

CROSS-DYEING: Process of dyeing fabric of mixed fibers with dye coloring only one set of fiber of fabric.

CUMMERBUND: Folded or pleated silk or rayon waistband worn with dinner jacket.

CUPRAMMONIUM: Rayon, from fibers of regenerated cellulose, solidified in solution of ammoniacal copper oxide. Produces fine-denier yarn.

CUSHION-FOOT SOCK: Sock with foot of terry knit or fleece for added comfort. Inside soles usually brushed wool.

CUT AND SEWN: Any article of apparel cut from fabric and sewn by machine or hand.

CUTAWAY: Coat for formal day wear in worsted or cashmere, one-button style with peak lapels, plain or braided edges, tapers from button closing to tails, which hang to bend of knee in back. Can be black or oxford gray.

CUTOFFS: Short shorts of a slack or jean fabric, most often with a ragged edge although some carry a neat cuff.

DACRON: Du Pont's trade name for its polyester fiber. Used in all types of men's apparel, either in worsted-like fiber or softer for knitted wear.

DARVAN: Brand name of manmade fiber by Celanese Corporation of America.

DECANTIZING: Finishing process employed on pressed woolen or worsted cloth. Pressure of steam through vacuum system sets fabric, increases luster and gives some protection against shrinkage; both wet and dry process.

DEERSKIN: Pebble-grained leather made from deer hide; gloves, leather goods.

DEERSTALKER: Cloth hat with visor in front and in back; also may have ear flap at side over crown.

DEMIBOOT: A short boot measuring anywhere from 6 inches high (slightly above the ankle) to 10 inches high (midcalf).

DEMIBOSOM: Short, stiff or pleated shirt bosom for semiformal or formal daytime wear; suitable for business.

DENIER: Unit of measure of filament yarn. Equals weight of single filament 400 meters in length. Indicates size or number of a filament or yarn. Higher deniers numbers show heavier yarn. Used in silk, rayon, nylon.

DENIM: Twill-weave cotton fabric with powdery tinge, obtained by using white filling yarns with colored warp yarns; sports, work clothing.

DERBY: Stiff-brimmed, hard, rounded-crown hat. Synonym for bowler.

DEVELOPED DYEING: Used on direct dye to alter shade of same color or to increase color resistance to sun and washing.

DIAGONAL WEAVE: Soft woolen fabric, woven in steep twill weave with pronounced twill line in wool or wool and rayon or cotton blends; suits, sportswear.

DINNER JACKET: Semiformal evening jacket, single- or double-breasted with peak lapels or shawl collar. Synonym for tuxedo.

DIP DYEING: Process employed on hosiery and other knit goods after knitting.

DOBBY: Small patterned weave, such as a dot or square, often in shirting type of fabric.

DOESKIN: Buffed inner side of doe, lamb or sheepskin; used for gloves and leather goods. Also made of wool; twill-woven rayon fabric; sportswear.

DONEGAL: Originally tweed hand-woven by Irish peasants; now machine-made tweed with colorful thick spots or slubs woven into fabric; suits, topcoats, sportswear.

DOUBLE-BREASTED: Jacket or coat cut to allow overlapping of several inches at front closing, with double row of buttons, one row to close.

DOUBLE KNIT: A jersey yarn knitted on a circular machine with a double set of needles. Double knits can be solid, patterned or textured, and in texture can go from very thin to broad corduroy-like effects.

DRAWN GRAIN: Finish in which leather grain is shrunken, shriveled or wrinkled. Used on leather goods and shoes.

DRAWSTRING: Tape, cord, braid running through tunnel to draw in to size of waist; pajamas, golf or ski jackets.

DRESS SHIRT: (1) Trade term to describe regular collar-attached shirts. (2) Shirt for formal evening wear with tailcoat, starched bosom, wing collar, single or French cuff. (3) Shirt for semi-formal evening wear with dinner jacket, fold collar, single or French cuffs, pleated bosom.

DRILL: Cotton fabric of diagonal weave running upward to left selvage; uniforms, heavy shirts, work clothes, sportswear.

DROP STITCH: In knitwear, simulated rib stitch made by omitting one needle from knitting so that when it rotates one stitch is dropped, giving open design.

DRY GOODS: Term includes piece goods, narrow yard goods and other textile items.

DUCK: Tightly woven cotton fabric similar to canvas with plain or rib weaves; work clothes, sportswear.

DUCK-BILL: Square-tip design of shoe.

DUFFEL COAT: A knee-length coat usually in a heavy tan or navy melton cloth, featuring a bucket hood, large flapped pockets, and cylindrical or horn-shaped buttons that fasten through a loop of rope instead of a buttonhole.

DUMMY: Wood of fabric-framed display unit built to resemble body contours. Used to display apparel accessories, suits, over-coats, etc.

DYEING: Process of coloring fibers or fabrics with either natural or synthetic dyes.

DYNEL: A synthetic staple fiber made from acrylonite and vinyl chloride, developed by Union Carbide and Carbon Corporation.

ECRU: Tan of shade of unbleached linen.

ELASTIQUE: Worsted suiting with steep double twill; uniforms, sportswear.

ELK LEATHER: Cattle hide leather of special tannage and finish; rugged appearance, used in sport shoes.

EMBROIDERY: Figure or ornamental design, done with needlework.

END-AND-END: Weave with alternate warp yarns of white and color, forming fine check; used in cotton chambray, broadcloths, oxfords for shirts and pajamas, underwear, sportswear.

ENGLISH DRAPE: Name commonly applied to men's jackets or outer coats which have extra fullness across chest to form flat wrinkles and similar fullness across shoulder blades; single- or double-breasted.

ENSEMBLE: Entire costume or items of apparel worn for an occasion or use and related in color, fabric and fashion rightness.

EPAULET: Shoulder strap or ornament, used on military uniforms, also on raincoats, sport shirts or jackets.

ESPADRILLE: Rope-soled beach and sport sandal with canvas uppers; originated by Spanish, French dock hands.

ETON JACKET: Short jacket with lapels, usually in boys' clothing.

FABRIC: Generic textile term meaning cloth, material, goods, etc. May be felt, woven, knitted or crocheted.

FACED CLOTH: All fabrics which feature separate warp or filling on back of goods.

FAILLE: Soft, slightly shiny, silk, rayon or cotton fabric in rib weave with flat cross-grain rib or cord made by using heavier yarns in filling than in warp; neckwear, lapels on evening clothes and other trimmings.

FASHION: Prevailing design, color and line in apparel and accessories in conventional usage at a given time.

FELT: Thick, firmly packed material made of wool, hair, fur or combination of matted fibers, pressed with moisture and heat; hats, sportswear trim, slippers.

FIBER: Smallest unit forming basic substance, filament or staple in manufacture of all fabrics; animal, vegetable or man-made.

FILAMENT RAYON: Continuous fiber of rayon made by viscose, acetate or cuprammonium process.

FILLING: (1) Yarn running crosswise in a woven fabric at right angles to warp yarn. (2) Term for sizing substances used to give fabric body, weight.

FINISHING: General term covering treatment of fabric for various surface effects or to improve, extend usefulness.

FLANNEL: Loosely woven, plaid or twill-weave fabric of woolen or worsted, spun rayon or spun rayon and wool blends. Unfinished or soft-napped surface; solid colors, stripes, checks, plaids. Wide varieties of weight and texture; suits, sportswear.

FLAT KNIT: Simple knit structure with vertical rows on face and crosswise bars on back.

FLAX: Flax plant fiber; spun into linen yarns, later woven into fabrics; all types of clothing, furnishings.

FLEECE: Fabric of soft, lofty surface and density.

FLY FRONT: Placket concealing button closure on coats, jackets, trousers.

FOLD COLLAR: Double shirt collar of turn-down style, attached or separate.

FORMAL: Type of apparel for full-dress occasions; tailcoat or tuxedo for evening, cutaway or oxford jacket outfit for daytime affairs.

FORTREL: Brand name of polyester fiber made by Celanese Corporation of America.

FORWARD COLLAR: Low-front shirt collar with stitching set back half-inch from edge.

FOULARD: (1) Twill-weave, lightweight printed silk or rayon fabric; neckwear, robes, mufflers, handkerchiefs. (2) Applies to certain types of small-pattern printed or woven lightweight fabric.

FOUR-IN-HAND: Type of necktie, knot, apron and end folding vertically.

FRENCH-BACK SERGE: Double-surfaced fabric with twill weave on face, satin weave on back; used in suits.

FRENCH CUFF: Double or turned-back cuff of shirt.

FRIAR'S CLOTH: A coarse drapery fabric in a basket weave. A trade name for monk's cloth, also called bishop's cloth.

FRIEZE: Heavy woolen overcoating with napped face; features double cloth with twill construction, available in spun rayon and wool combination.

FROG: Stitched-on braid forming looped design at buttonholes; used on lounging pajamas and nightwear.

FRONTIER PANTS: Trim-fitting pants or slacks with tapered lines, as first worn by wranglers or ranchers.

FULL-FASHIONED: Flat-knit process, features adding and reducing stitches for shaping to conform to body lines when seamed; used in hose, sweaters, underwear.

FULLING: A process in the finishing of woolen cloth. The cloth is dampened and beaten under heat, obscuring the weave.

FUSED COLLAR: Processed collar with specially prepared interlining laminated to outer layers of shirting to minimize wilting and wrinkling.

GABARDINE: Tightly woven worsted cotton, rayon or blended fabric showing steep twill. May be made of single- or two-ply yarns. In solid colors; all types of clothing, sportswear.

GABERDINE: A loose mantle or coat worn by medieval workers.

GALATEA: Sturdy, printed twill cotton fabric used in beachwear and sports clothing.

GALOSH: Overshoe of rubber or other material.

GAUGE: (1) Standard of measure of thickness or fineness of a knitted fabric, dependent upon number of needles in given unit of space. (2) A shoe that has leather loops instead of eyelets—a motif derived from the heavy shoes worn in nineteenth-century Scotland and revived in the 1960s via lightweight models and boots.

GAUNTLET: Extra-length glove with wrist portion slanting out to a flare.

GILLIE: Tongueless oxford, laced across instep and tied around ankle.

GINGHAM: Plain-weave cotton fabric in checks, stripes or plaids; sportswear.

GLEN PLAID: See Glenurquhart.

GLENURQUHART: Scottish clan plaid with overplaid in another shade or color formed by groups of lines crossing at right angles to form boxlike design; design in tweeds and other fabrics used for suitings, sportswear.

GOATSKIN: Pebble-grain leather made from goat hide; sport gloves, leather goods.

GORE SHOE: House-type slipper or shoe with elasticized sides or front.

GRAINED LEATHER: Finished by boarding, embossing or printing to produce special surface pattern.

GRANDRELLE: Ply yarn spun of strands of different colors into shirting or pajamas fabrics to produce heather effect in stripe and allover pattern.

GRANITE CLOTH: Hard-finished woolen fabric of twisted yarn giving rough, pebbled surface; suitings, sportswear.

GRASS CLOTH: Loosely woven fabric made in the Orient of grass, ramie or vegetable fibers; used in natural brown color, bleached or dyed, for sportswear.

GRAY OR GREIGE GOODS: General term applied to all fabrics prior to bleaching, dyeing or finishing.

GRENADINE: Gauzelike neckwear fabric in which threads cross each other from side to side.

GRENFELL CLOTH: Closely woven cloth originally used on the Grenfell Mission in Labrador.

GROSGRAIN: Closely woven, corded fabric of silk or rayon, sometimes with cotton filling; neckwear, trimming on evening clothes, accessories.

GUARD'S COAT: Long, dark-colored overcoat with half belt, inverted center pleat and deep folds at sides in back.

GUAYABERA SHIRT: A jacket shirt with four pockets worn originally by natives of Caribbean islands.

GUN CLUB CHECK: Even check pattern with alternating rows of checks in different colors; design most frequently seen in worsted, flannel, tweeds.

GUN FLAP: An extra piece of cloth for reinforcement at the shoulder on a trench coat. A style detail on garments for civilian wear.

GUN METAL: Dark gray shade, similar to that of metal of gun barrel.

GUSSET: Insert of fabric or leather at seams of garments to prevent ripping and to allow extra freedom of action. Usually triangular in shape.

HACKING JACKET: Riding coat, longer than regular sport coat, slight flare at bottom, deep side or center vent, slanting pockets, change pocket on right side above lower pocket.

HAIRCLOTH: Wiry cotton fabric made with horsehair or mohair filling; used for stiffening.

HAIRLINE STRIPE: Striped design woven in one-thread thickness in worsteds, other fabrics.

HANDKERCHIEF LINEN: Plain-weave, sheer, fine linen.

HAND-PICKED: Hand-stitching at the edges of a jacket, lapels, pockets, etc.

HAND-ROLLED: Edge rolled and sewn by hand, as in a handkerchief, scarf, etc.

HAND-WOVEN OR HAND-LOOMED: Descriptive of a fabric, woolen or other type, woven on a hand loom.

HANK: Skein of yarn or thread of a measured length.

HARRIS TWEED: Trade name for an imported tweed, made of virgin wool from Scottish Highlands, and spun, dyed and hand-woven by islanders in Harris and other Outer Hebrides Islands.

HAWAIIAN PRINTS: Floral motifs printed on cotton and rayon or silk fabrics with plain-weave construction; sportswear.

HEAD END: Beginning of a new piece of cloth, usually bearing identification marks.

HEATHER MIXTURE: Combination of colors in fibers giving blended color appearance; used mainly in tweeds, other woolen fabrics.

HELMET: Stiff head covering with rounded crown, medium-width brim with downward slope all around.

HERRINGBONE TWILL: Broken-twill weave with zigzag effect produced by alternating the direction of the twill. Similar to chevron weave; suits, topcoats, overcoats, sportswear.

HIGH FASHION: A new fashion in any type of apparel which has limited but selective acceptance.

HIGH SILK HAT: Shiny, pressed-silk, plush hat with curled brim; worn with tailcoat; formal day, evening wear.

HOMBURG: Soft, felt hat with stiff curled brim and tapered crown; black or midnight blue with dinner jacket for semiformal wear; worn for day wear in other colors.

HOMESPUN: Loosely woven woolen fabric originally made by hand, now duplicated by machine in cotton, rayon or wool.

Plain weave shows coarse yarns. Stock dyed in plain or nubbed effects.

HOPSACKING: Coarse, open-weave fabric of cotton or woolen yarns; has meshlike appearance; suitings, sportswear.

HORSEHIDE: Tough durable skin of horse; utility jackets, leather goods, work gloves, shoes.

HOUNDSTOOTH CHECK: Broken-design check simulating canine teeth; used in woolen, worsted, cotton, rayon fabrics.

HUARACHES: Braided leather sport shoes with sling back. Mexican peasant origin.

HUNTER'S PINK: Traditional bright scarlet coat color worn as formal hunting garb. Fabric in that color often referred to by same name.

HUNTING CAP: Round-crown cap with short visor and reinforcement.

HYMO FABRIC: A blend of mohair, to reinforce lapels and body of coat.

IN-AND-OUTER: Tailless sport shirt worn outside or inside shorts or slacks.

INDIA PRINT: Cotton printed in a characteristic native pattern, usually hand blocked in high colors.

INGRAIN: Fabrics constructed of yarns dyed before knitting or weaving.

INITIAL MARKUP: Difference between cost and retail value of total merchandise handled during period, expressed as percentage of retail value.

INSEAM: (1) Glove manufacturing term: glove stitched while inside out and turned to put on inside. (2) Inseam measurement of trousers: measurement from crotch to bottom of trouser.

INSIGNIA: Emblem or badge for distinction, such as a club emblem on blazer.

INSOLE: Section of shoes between welt and outsole.

INTERLINING: Layer of cloth between lining and outer fabric.

INVERNESS: Coat with elbow-length cape attached, single-breasted, with peak or notch lapel. Worn for country, sports in tweed; dark colors for formal wear.

IRIDESCENT: Having changing colors, as in a fabric with different-colored filling and warp yarns.

IRISH LINEN: Fine, lightweight linen woven of Irish flax; hand-kerchiefs, shirts.

ITALIAN CLOTH: Cotton- or wool-backed satin fabric used chiefly for coat and suit linings. Similar to Venetian cloth.

JACQUARD: Method of achieving intricate pattern and color effects on fabric through weaving and/or knitting. Accomplished through controlled needle selection and movement on flatbed machine or loom; ties, robes, pajamas, shirts, sportswear.

JEAN: A twill fabric used in work clothing. Jeans: slacks made of this fabric.

JERSEY: Plain-knitted fabric with faint rib on one side; wool, cotton or rayon or combined with other fibers; has elasticity; underwear, sport shirts, sportswear.

JIPIJAPA: (1) Synonym for *toquilla*. Strong fiber from jipijapa leaves woven into fine straw for Panama hats. (2) Wide-brimmed planter's-type hat.

JODHPUR BOOT: Riding shoe extending above ankle, fastening with strap.

JODHPURS: Ankle-length riding trousers wide across hips, tapering to knees, fitting leg closely from knee to ankle; cuff at bottom. Worn with low jodhpur boots.

KEMP: Short-staple, coarse hair of wool.

KHAKI: (1) Color of brown, red, yellow combination resembling withered leaves of African khaki bush. (2) General term for warp twills and drills dyed to this shade; uniforms, sportswear, work clothes.

KIDSKIN: Soft, pliable, tight-grain skin of young goat; gloves, shoes, slippers, leather goods.

KILTIE TONGUE: Fringed tongue overlapping laces and instep of shoe.

KNICKERS: Short for knickerbockers, type of trousers with full-ness confined in a band at the knee; sportswear.

KNOP: Novelty yarn featuring vivid-colored lumps of fiber inter-spersed throughout basic fibers in yarn. Also identified as knopped or knop yarn.

KODEL: Brand name of polyester fiber made by Eastman Chemical Company.

LAMB'S WOOL: Fabric of soft wool fibers of lambs.

LAMÉ: Silk or rayon fabric woven in designs with flat metal threads which form either the background or the pattern, most often done in either silver or gold.

LAMINATED FABRIC: Fabric joined in layers with resin acetate or other adhesives as in fused collars.

LAPEL: Facing of jacket or coat front. Portion of coat front which turns back to join with collar.

LAST: Wooden form over which shoes are made.

LAWN: Cotton fabric, light, thin-textured, of combed or corded yarn; handkerchiefs.

LEGHORN: Finely plaited straw; wheat fibers imported from Italy, woven into hats.

LEI: Wreath of flowers in Hawaii; feather band for hats.

LENO: Loose, open weave of fabric.

LIGNE: French unit of measurement to determine width of hatband or hat binding. Ligne equals $\frac{1}{11}$ of an inch.

LINEN: Smooth-surfaced, flax-fibered fabric or yarn; handkerchiefs, dress shirts, underwear, sportswear.

LINEN MESH: Open-weave fabric, strong, easily washable, used for shirts, underwear.

LINKS-AND-LINKS: Type of purl stitching in knitting.

LINTERS: Short cotton fibers which adhere to cottonseed after first ginning; used for manufacture of cellulose sheets in making rayon.

LISLE: Fabric of fine, hard-twisted, long-staple cotton thread, of two or more ply yarns; hosiery, underwear, sport shirts.

LLAMA: Underfleece of llama (species of camel). Often combined with wool in overcoating.

LONG-ROLL COLLAR: Low-front collar on shirts having 3¾-to-4-inch points.

LONG-STAPLE COTTON: Fiber having length not less than 1⅛ inches.

LOUNGE SUIT: Sack suit with double- or single-breasted jacket in soft fabric for business wear.

LOVAT: Heather mixture of dull blue or dull green combined with tan or gray. Lovat describes color obtained by mixture, does not refer to particular fabric.

LOW-SLOPE COLLAR: Attached collar on which upper line has forward slope and neckband is set low.

LUMBERJACK SHIRT: Plaid wool, cotton or rayon-blend fabric shirt used as a work shirt or for winter sportswear. Originally worn by Canadian lumberjacks.

LYCRA: A spandex fiber of the polyester type, manufactured by Du Pont; has elastic and shape-retaining qualities.

MACCLESFIELD: Rough, open weave, usually in small, compact, overall patterns in subdued colors. Term refers to type of pattern rather than weave. Used interchangeably with Spitalfields. Names derived from districts in England where they were originally woven; neckwear.

MACKINAW: Short, heavy outdoor coat. Sometimes called lumberman's jacket. Usually in bright plaids, wool fleece.

MACKINTOSH: Waterproof coat.

MADDER: Type of vegetable dyestuff for fabrics; soft-tone printed fabrics for neckwear or sportswear; known as madder prints.

MADRAS: Cotton or spun-rayon fabric with woven stripe, check or cord effect patterns, of same fabric color or in contrast.

MARL: Two-tone yarn which produces a heatherlike mixture in fabric; socks, sweaters.

MAT FINISH: Dull, flat finish applied to leather in shoes, luggage, leather accessories.

MEDALLION: Perforated pattern punched in center of shoe tips.

MELTON: Compact, heavily felted woolen fabric, usually of plain weave with short-napped surface; overcoats, sportswear.

MERCERIZING: Treatment of cotton using caustic soda at low temperature to make fabric or yarn stronger, more lustrous, more absorbent and more acceptable to dye. Permanent finish.

MERINO: Wool from merino sheep woven into soft fabric resembling cashmere; used in suitings, coatings, sportswear.

MESH FABRICS: Knitted or woven fabric with open-mesh texture of cotton, silk, wool, linen, rayon or combinations; sportswear, underwear.

MILAN: Closely braided fine fibers for summer hats.

MILDEW-RESISTANT: Quality of fabric imparted by chemical treatment to resist mildew, mold.

MILL ENDS: Remnants or short lengths of fabric.

MITTEN: Hand covering with two compartments, one for thumb and one for four other fingers and hand.

MOCCASIN: Sport shoe on which one piece of leather cradling vamp is hand-sewn to vamp. Ball strap with cutout design stitched to vamp and upper. Sole attached to leather cradling.

MOCHA: Skin of haired sheep; soft velvet finish, close texture; gloves.

MOGADOR: Heavily corded tie silk with close-packed threads, extremely firm texture; usually features vividly colored stripes.

MOHAIR: Smooth, glossy fabric from fiber of Angora goat; coats, linings, etc.

MOIRÉ: Watered effect on faille, taffeta or acetate rayon fabrics made by engraved rollers; neckwear, vests, trimming on evening wear, robes.

MOLESKIN CLOTH: Cotton-filled sateen fabric backed with thick nap resembling fur; used for semidress pants, lined coats.

MONK-FRONT SHOE: A plain-toe shoe with strap over instep and buckle at side.

MORDANT: Chemical used in some textile-dyeing processes to increase affinity between fiber and dye.

MOROCCO: Goatskin leather with pebbled grain; leather goods, accessories.

MOUTON: Short- or medium-length dense-pile fur featured in dyed shades with good wearing quality; sportswear, outerwear.

MUKLUK: Alaskan Eskimo boot of sealskin with the fur side out; worn for after-ski and casual purposes.

MULES: Counterless house slippers.

MULL: Lightweight sheer cotton or other fabric.

MUSLIN: Firm cotton cloth with plain weave; one of the oldest staple cotton cloths; underwear, shirts.

NAINSOOK: Plain-woven fabric of fine, soft cotton; better-grade underwear and pajamas.

NAPPING: Finishing process to raise fibers of cloth to surface by means of revolving cylinders.

NECKBAND SHIRT: Standard type finished with buttonholes in front and back of neckband, worn with separate collar.

NECKERCHIEF: A square of cotton, silk or other fabric for wear around the neck.

NOIL: Short-yarn fiber obtained during combing and carding operation mixed with longer fiber in woolen and worsted manufacture.

NORFOLK JACKET: Belted jacket with yoke at back and front of shoulders, box pleats extending from yoke to waist, two in front and one in back, or to bottom of jacket.

NOTCHED LAPEL: Fairly wide, V-shaped opening at outside edge of seam between collar and lapel.

NYLON: Synthetic textile yarn; toughness, strength, washability, quick drying, elasticity, resistance to mildew and insects claimed as advantages. Used alone or blended with other fibers in hosiery, underwear, shirts, sportswear.

OBSOLESCENCE: Process of going out of use or fashion; becoming outmoded; loss in value of merchandise or fixed assets caused by change in fashion or new trends.

OILED SILK: Pliable, transparent silk fabric, waterproofed by immersion in boiled linseed oil and dried; used in some rainwear.

OILSKIN: Waterproof cotton raincoat processed with several coatings of oil.

OLIVE: Soft green shade of yellowish cast similar to that of unripe olive.

OMBRÉ: Fashion term for shaded or graduated color in striped effect; neckwear, pajamas.

OPERA HAT: Dull silk or rayon collapsible hat with curled brim; formal, semiformal evening wear.

ORLON: Du Pont's trade name for its acrylic fiber, manufactured from polyacrylonitrile.

OSTRICH LEATHER: South African in origin; identified by quill holes in finished leather; leather luggage, accessories.

OTTOMAN: Densely woven fabric with crosswise ribs; in silk, used for neckwear.

OUTING FLANNEL: Plain- or twill-weave cotton fabric napped on both sides; sleepwear.

OVERPLAID: Double plaid; cloth in which weave or color effect is arranged in blocks of different sizes one over the other; suitings, sportswear.

OXFORD: Low-cut shoe with lacing of three or more eyelets over instep; made in wing-tip, blucher, brogue and gillie styles.

OXFORD SHIRTING: Modified plain- or basket-weave cotton fabric; originated in Oxford, England; shirts, sportswear, heavy grades used in summer suitings, sportswear.

OYSTER WHITE: Off-white shade in rainwear.

PAISLEY: Printed, woven designs found in Kashmirian shawls, adapted to neckwear, mufflers, sportswear.

PAJAMA: Nightwear suit consisting of coat or middy shirt and trousers; adapted for lounging.

PALM BEACH CLOTH: Trade name for summer suiting; controlled by the Palm Beach Company.

PANAMA: Fine, hand-plaited straw made from moistened fibers of the *toquilla* or fiber from the leaves of the jipijapa plant. From Ecuador, Peru, Colombia.

PANNE SATIN: High-lustered silk or rayon satin used as trim for evening wear, top hats.

PARCHMENT: Very pale tan shade for fabrics.

PARKA: Hooded garment with sleeves usually in water-repellent fabrics for outdoor winter sports, work.

PATCH POCKET: Pocket stitched on the outside of a garment.

PEA JACKET: Short blue naval coat; also adapted for civilian wear.

PEAKED LAPEL: Lapel of jacket or coat which comes to a point at outer edge, with narrow spacing between lapel and bottom of collar.

PEBBLE GRAIN: Irregular texture of leather achieved by embossing surface.

PEBBLE WEAVE: Fabric woven of shrunken, twisted yarns.

PECCARY: Pigskin obtained from wild boar; fine-grained; gloves, leather goods.

PENCIL STRIPE: A men's suiting with stripes two or three warps wide in contrasting color to the ground or basic fabric.

PERCALE: Medium-weight plain or printed cotton fabric with firm, plain weave, smooth finish; shirts, pajamas, sportswear.

PERCALINE: Glazed or moiréd cotton lining fabric.

PICK: Single-filling thread which interlaces with warp, a series of which form a woven fabric.

PICK-AND-PICK: Loom mechanism in which single picks from different shuttles are inserted in regular succession.

PICOT: Purl or small loop woven on edge of fabrics. Sometimes made with a hemstitching machine.

PIECE-DYED: Fabric dyed after weaving.

PIECE GOODS: Broad goods sold generally by the yard.

PIGSKIN: Coarse, pebble-grained leather, dark bristle pits; gloves, leather goods of all kinds.

PILE: Cut or uncut loops forming surface of a fabric; can be made in variation of twill, raised nap or plain weave.

PILLING: The formation of little fuzz balls on the surface of a fabric caused by the rubbing off of loose ends of the fiber.

PIMA COTTON: Fine American cotton grown in the Southwest.

PINCHECK: End-and-end-weave fabric with fine check made with alternating colored yarns, usually woven; shirts, suits, sportswear.

PINKING: Process of cutting edges of fabric in sawtooth pattern to prevent fraying.

PIN SEAL: Leather tanned from sealskins with grain pattern retained; often imitated by embossing process; gloves, accessories.

PIQUÉ: Narrow-waled, woven cotton fabric, sometimes of rayon or silk. Wales run lengthwise or form fine honeycomb weave called waffle piqué; shirts, accessories for evening wear, sportswear. Can be simulated in knit construction.

PITH HELMET: Light pith hat for wear in hot-weather areas.

PLAID: Bar patterns of different colors crossed to form varied squares; used in all fabrics.

PLAIN WEAVE: Basic weave in which filling yarns pass over and under warp yarns, alternating each row; used in all fabrics.

PLAITING: Alternate placing of one colored yarn or fiber over another. Term used in knitting and weaving.

PLEATED BOSOM: Shirt front for semiformal evening, formal or semiformal day wear, made with pleats of identical or varying widths, starched or soft.

PLY: Measurement of yarns formed by twisting together more than one single strand.

POINTED-END TIE: Straight-cut bow tie with pointed ends.

POINTING AND SILKING: Type of stitching on back of glove to form raised ridges.

POINTS: The distance from the shirt neckband to the collar tips.

POKE COLLAR: Standing collar for formal wear.

POLO COAT: Topcoat, overcoat in camel's hair or other soft fabrics, double-breasted, with half or full belt, patch pockets, wide-welt seams and edges, set-in or raglan sleeves.

POLO SHIRT: Lightweight knit shirt with or without collar, featuring short opening at neck; active sportswear.

POLYESTER: Generic term for fiber, a condensation of polymer obtained from ethylene glycol and terephthalic acid. Trade names: Dacron, Vycron, Fortrel, Kodel.

PONGEE: Rough-woven, thin, natural-colored silk fabric; summer suits, underwear, pajamas, sportswear.

POPLIN: Fabric woven on grosgrain principle on cotton, silk or rayon with wool filling, or may be of nylon; similar to broadcloth but of heavier rib; shirts, coats, suits, underwear, pajamas.

PORKPIE: Sport hat in felt or fabric having flat-top, low, telescope crown. (See Telescope Crown.)

POROMERIC MATERIAL: A urethane polymer material reinforced with polyester, it attracted considerable attention in the sixties as a manmade material for shoe uppers. "Corfam," the most widely promoted of these materials, was, however, taken off the market by Du Pont in 1971.

PRINCE ALBERT: Frock coat, named after Prince Albert of England.

PRINT: Term used to designate fabrics with applied designs of dye on roller, blocks or screens by printing.

PRIXSEAM (P.X.M.): Outseam on glove, stitched with machine needle moving horizontally instead of vertically, to form even edge.

PUGREE: Straw-hat band fashioned originally in India; usually of soft, pleated fabric, plain or patterned.

PULLOVER: Sweater or shirt with or without sleeves which has no complete front opening and must be pulled on over the head.

PUMP: Low-cut shoe without lacing or strap, with ornamental

grosgrain ribbon bow at front; in patent leather, dull calf for formal evening wear.

PURE DYE: Term applied to colored silk that has no metallic weighting.

PURL: Knit stitch with horizontal ridges on both sides of fabric.

RACK STITCH: Knit stitch giving herringbone effect with ribbed back; sweaters, sportswear.

RAFFIA: Light-colored fiber made of leaves of raffia palm.

RAGLAN: Loose topcoat with sleeves cut so that sleeve seam runs from armhole to neck in front and back.

RAMIE: Similar to flax; originally from eastern Asiatic plant, now grown in southern United States; sportswear.

RATINÉ: Loose, plain-woven fabric with nubby, uneven surface made of knotty yarns; sportswear.

RAYON: (1) Generic term for manufactured textile fiber or yarn produced chemically from regenerated cellulose and containing an amount of nonregenerated cellulose fiber-forming material. (2) A term for threads of fabrics manufactured under viscose, acetate, cuprammonium nitrocellulose or other processes.

REEFER: Short, single- or double-breasted, fitted, tailored overcoat.

REP (REPP): Corded fabric with pronounced crosswise rib, similar to poplin; of rayon, silk, cotton, wool or mixture; furnishings, sportswear.

REPROCESSED WOOL: Wool fibers which have been previously woven, knitted or manufactured, never put to use, then unraveled, reduced to fiber and spun and rewoven into fabric.

REUSED WOOL: Wool fibers which have been previously manufactured and used by consumers, reduced to fiber stage and rewoven.

REVERSE KNIT: Flat or plain knit used inside out for dull texture in sweaters, socks.

REVERSE TWIST: Used in describing fabric of yarns spun counterclockwise woven with other yarns spun clockwise. This creates a special pattern.

REVERSIBLE: Outer coat of reversible fabric or of two different fabrics that can be worn with either side out.

RIB KNIT: Fabric with lengthwise knit on both sides; knit on two sets of opposed needles working together.

RICKRACK: Flat braid in zigzag form; sometimes used as trim on pajamas.

ROMAINE: Semisheer fabric of creped yarn; woven of rayon or wool; used in better-quality shirts, pajamas.

S TWIST: Direction of twist of yarn of cord similar to S spiral.

SABOTS: Wooden-sole slip-on shoes for casual wear; also worn by European peasants.

SADDLE LEATHER: Vegetable-tanned cowhide; belts, suspenders, leather goods, sport shoes.

SADDLE OXFORD: Laced shoe with contrasting band of leather across instep.

SADDLE SHOULDER: A version of the raglan sleeve, but instead of converging at the collar, the seams extend to it, remaining parallel.

SADDLE STITCH: Regular, widely spaced stitch done by hand or resembling hand stitch, using heavy thread; gloves, leather goods.

SANDAL: Low, open-front shoe with crossed straps and buckle fastenings.

SANFORIZED: Trademark for process of shrinkage control of fabrics.

SASSE YARN: Spun-rayon yarn made of viscose staple fiber.

SATEEN: Satin-weave cotton fabric used primarily for linings; usually mercerized.

SATIN: Fabric with glasslike effect of smoothness on surface and dull back; finish produced by running fabric through hot cylinders; neckwear, trimming on evening wear, robes.

SAXONY: Woolen suiting fabric resembling unfinished worsted, slightly napped surface, usually twill weave; in solid colors, mixtures and chalk stripes. Also closely twisted fine yarn used in knitting.

SCOTCHGARD: Trademark of MMM of process for stain resistance and water-repellency of fabrics.

SCOURING: Freeing wool of dirt, natural grease, dry perspiration.

SEERSUCKER: Cotton, rayon or silk fabric with crinkled stripes made by weaving warp threads slack and tight. Launders without ironing. Available plain, printed or cross-dyed for suits, pajamas, robes, shirts.

SELVAGE (SELVEDGE): Extreme outside edge of cloth woven in special yarn for reinforcement.

SENNIT: (1) Flat straw plaited in angles; finished in natural color. (2) Stiff straw hat with flat brim in sailor shape.

SERGE: Twill-weave worsted fabric with smooth surface, diagonal rib on both sides of fabric. Also available in spun rayon, wool, cotton or blends; suits, sportswear.

SHANK: Tempered steel or flexible leather, extending from fore part of heel of shoe, fitting under arch to support it.

SHANTUNG: Silk or rayon fabric similar to pongee with nubby surface; suits, sportswear.

SHARKSKIN: (1) Smooth-surfaced fabric in plain weave of continuous rayon yarns in warp and filling; neckwear, sportswear. (2) Clear-faced worsted fabric of twill weave usually with nailhead design; suits.

SHAWL COLLAR: Long, soft-rolling lapel, without peaks or indentations at gorge; dinner jackets, robes.

SHEARLING: Lamb or sheepskin tanned with wool still adhering to the skin; used as lining in coats, snowsuits, gloves.

SHEPHERD'S CHECK: Twill-weave fabric with small, even checks in contrasting colors; made in wool, rayon or blends; sportswear, neckwear.

SHETLAND: Applied only to wool from sheep raised in Shetland Isles off Scotland. Extremely lightweight and warm.

SHIRTING: Fabric identification used for cloth in manufacture of shirts.

SHORT-ROUNDED COLLAR: Shirt collar with rounded points.

SHRUNKEN CALF: Calfskin with small patterns created by shrinking the hide.

SILK: Natural fiber from cocoon of silkworm, with native resiliency to resist wrinkling.

SILK FLOSS: Short fibers of tangled waste silk.

SINGLE-BREASTED: Jacket with one-, two-, or three-button closing or outer coat with three-to-five-button closing, neither with more than an inch overlap; buttons set near the edge of opening.

SINGLE CUFF: An attached starched shirt cuff of single thickness, worn with cuff links.

SIX BY THREE RIB: Six ribs of knitting on outside of fabric separated by three ribs in reverse.

SIZING: Finishing process to add strength, smoothness, stiffness, weight to yarn or fabric.

SKI BOOT: High shoe with squared tip, walled sides, heavily reinforced sole to which skis are clamped.

SLACKS: Loose-fitting trousers of wool, worsted, cotton, rayon or blends worn separately or in combinations for sportswear.

SLACK SUIT: Suit of matching or contrasting colors, consisting of trousers and jacket or shirt; beach and sportswear.

SLEAZY: Term describing thin, open-mesh fabric which lacks firmness.

SLEEP COAT: Coat for nightwear reaching knee or below, half- or full-length sleeve, generally belted; cotton, rayon.

SLEY: Identification for number of warp ends per inch woven into cloth.

SLICKER: Oiled cotton or silk raincoat with standing collar; corduroy lined.

SLIDE FASTENER: Flexible-edge closing device with interlocking components opened or closed by slide puller. Made of metal or synthetics.

SLOPE: The height of the shirt collar on the neck. Usually there's a choice among regular, high or low slope and all collar styles are customarily available in each of these constructions.

SLOTTED COLLAR: Shirt collar which features stays on underside of collar fronts to keep ends from curling.

SNAP-BRIM HAT: Hat in felt, straw or fabric with brim turned down in front, up in back.

SNAP FASTENER: Springlike closure in two parts, slotted circular metal disk overlapped on metal stud; sewed on or riveted through fabric; underwear, sportswear, gloves.

SNEAKER: Canvas oxford with rubber sole and heel; tennis, other sports.

SOMBRERO: Mexican hat with tall crown and wide rolling brim.

SOUTACHE: Herringbone-effect, narrow rounded braid; used for trimming robes, sportswear.

SPINDLE: The long, thin rod used for twisting and holding the spun thread when spinning on a wheel or machine.

SPINNING: Act of drawing and twisting fibers together to produce thread or yarn.

SPITALFIELDS: See Macclesfield.

SPLIT SHAWL: Popular in outercoats designed for casual wear, this is an especially dashing collar that extends in an uninterrupted line completely around the neck and down to the coat's top button, but then comes separated into an upper and lower portion at the collarbone.

SPONGING: Steaming woolen piece goods by passing under perforated cylinders before making into garments.

SPOT-AND-STAIN-RESISTANT: Fabric specially treated before garment manfacturing to resist stains.

SPREAD: The measurement between the collar tips of a shirt.

SPUN GLASS: Fine fibers or filaments formed from glass batch of sand, limestone and other minerals melted, refined and drawn. Characterized by flexibility, fire resistance, high water resistance, shrinkage and mildew resistance; used as interlining.

SPUN LINEN: Hand-woven fabric, used for fine-quality handkerchiefs, neckwear.

SPUN RAYON: Short lengths of viscose, acetate or cuprammonium staple rayon fiber twisted together into yarn for fabric weaving. Blended with other yarns for suiting and overcoats.

SPUN SILK: Yarn, fabric made from short silk fibers which cannot be reeled.

STAPLE: Term describing the average length of any fiber.

STARCHED BOSOM: Shirt for formal wear with two or three thicknesses of fabric on set-in bosom. One-, two- and three-stud closure. Usually made of piqué.

STUDS: Shirt fastenings used for formal, semiformal wear, usually of pearl, cabochon, colored stones or gold.

SUEDE: (1) Buffed inner side of almost all leathers. Used in gloves, shoes and all types of leather goods. (2) Finish on woven or knitted fabrics which produces light chamois nap.

SUITING: General term applied to all fabrics used in manufacture of suits and coats.

SURAH: Soft, twilled silk or sometimes rayon fabric; ties and mufflers.

SWATCH: Small unit of cloth as sample of any textile fabric; used to show pattern or design in clothing and accessory items available on special order.

SYL-MER: Silicone finish of durable water-repellency, made by Dow Corning Corporation.

SYNTHETIC LEATHER: Cellulose, rubber, rubber composition, fiberboard, coated fabric, coated paper and pasteboard; resembles leather.

TAB COLLAR: Shirt collar, points of which are held in place by tabs fastened to neckband or together.

TAILCOAT: Evening coat with tails beginning at waist seam, extending to side seams and tapering in back to bend of knee. Coat extends to waist in front, does not button. Grosgrain or satin facing on lapels; midnight blue or black. Formal evening wear with white tie only.

TANNING: Process of preparing, converting raw hides into finished leathers.

TARLATAN: Open-mesh, transparent muslin; thin-textured; used as stiffening in garments.

TARTAN: Original Scottish plaids woven into woolen, worsted or spun rayon in box designs and colors of Highland clans; neckwear, sportswear.

TATTERSALL: Overcheck pattern formed by vertical and horizontal lines in one-, two- or three-color effects; used in flannels, other wool fabrics, cottons, rayons; sportswear.

TELESCOPE CROWN: Crown of hat creased at even height, flat top.

TENNIS SHOE: Canvas oxford with rubber sole and heel.

TERRY: Cotton fabric, highly absorbent, looped on one or both sides; beachwear, beach robes.

THREAD: Ply yarn with high number of turns or twists per inch.

Often waxed, coated or treated in some special way to work smoothly.

TIE BAR: Ornamental fastening to hold tie in place against shirt placket; usually chain, pin, clip.

TIE DYEING: Hand process, achieved by tightly tying parts of fabric in place so that joined parts do not take dye.

TIE SILK: Fine-quality silk fabric similar to foulard; neckties, lightweight robes.

TIED AND DYED: Pattern based on tie dyeing; neckwear.

TOE BOX: Stiff leather shell placed between lining and tip to ensure permanent shape to front of shoe.

TONGUE: Piece of leather attached to throat of vamp on laced shoe, extends upward under lacing.

TOPCOAT: Lightweight overcoat; fabrics of fourteen to eighteen ounces to linear yard.

TRENCH COAT: Processed gabardine outer coat modeled from English officers' coats, World War I. Original had shoulder flaps, reinforced extra-processed lining. Civilian counterpart is same style but adapted for less rigorous needs.

TREWS: Close-fitting knitted garment (trousers and stockings) worn by Scotsmen under kilts. Also used as name for close-fitting trousers.

TRICOT: Synonym for jersey. Warp-knit fabric with double-faced rib; face of cloth features rib knitting, underside ribs run crosswise; underwear, sportswear, beachwear, gloves.

TRICOTINE: Synonym for fabric similar to gabardine with double-twill weave; identified as cavalry twill; suiting, sportswear.

TROPICAL WORSTED: Lightweight suiting for summer wear made in various weaves; two-ply worsted yarns in warp and filling or may be single-ply; suiting, sportswear.

TUBULAR FABRICS: Any seamless fabric woven or knitted in tubular form; primarily in underwear and socks.

TURTLENECK SWEATER: Knitted garment with turned-over collar, usually ribbed without front opening, covering neck.

TUSCAN: Fine, yellow straw, woven from bleached wheat stalks grown in Italy, woven in lacelike designs for straw hats.

TUXEDO: Synonym for dinner jacket.

TWEED: Rough-surfaced, coarse wool fabric of plain or twill weave in patterns, checks or plaids; first made by weavers on Tweed River in Scotland; clothing, sportswear.

TWILL: A basic weave; features distinct diagonal line; used in all fabrics.

TWIST: Turn of ply or thread in yarn for fabric manufacture.

TYROLEAN HAT: Rough-fabric felt or velour hat with tapered crown and narrow brim, cord band and brush at side; sports or country wear.

UNCONSTRUCTED SUIT: An umbrella term for the "casual suit" or "easy suit," whose basic characteristics are the absence of shoulder padding, lining and any hand tailoring.

UNFINISHED WORSTED: Fabric of medium-twisted worsted yarn; twill weave concealed by slightly napped surface; patterns or plain; suits, topcoats.

ULSTER: Heavy, long, loose-fitting overcoat with half or full belt, double-breasted, deep convertible collar.

UPLAND COTTON: General classification given all short-staple cotton grown in southern part of United States.

V NECK: Garment neckline which reaches V point on front.

VAMP: The section of the shoe that lies between the toe and the instep.

VAT DYE: Insoluble dye reduced in application to soluble form. Placed on fiber, then oxidized to soluble form. High resistance to washing and sunlight.

VEGETABLE FIBERS: Classification given all fabric or yarn fibers originating from vegetables, flax, cotton, ramie.

VELOUR: Closely woven, smooth fabric with short, thick pile; made of cotton, wool or spun rayon and wool blends; used in outer coating and in felt for hats.

VELVET: Fabric featuring soft, thick, short-pile surface of silk or rayon with cotton back; also all silk or all cotton.

VELVETEEN: Cotton filling fabric with short, close pile, made to simulate velvet.

VENETIAN CLOTH: Cotton or wool fabric, warp-faced, smooth-textured; in cotton, used for linings; in wool, used for topcoats, suits, sportswear.

VENT: Tailoring term meaning a center or side slit on bottom of coat or jacket.

VEREL: The modacrylic staple fiber, manufactured by Eastman Chemical Company.

VICARA: Trade name for synthetic fabric, very soft and cashmere-like in appearance, made by Virginia-Carolina Chemical Corporation.

VICUÑA: Soft fabric made from wool of vicuña, an animal similar to the llama. Considered finest of wool. Used in fabrics for evening wear, sportswear, suits; woven into fine sweaters.

VIGOUREX: Process of printing worsted fibers before spinning to give mixed color effect. Identified with worsted fabric which shows light and dark effects through use of this yarn.

VIRGIN WOOL: Wool which has not previously been made into yarn or fabric, or used for any other purpose.

VISCOSE RAYON: Rayon filaments made of regenerated cellulose coagulated from solution of cellulose xanthate.

VIYELLA: Brand name for fabrics woven or knitted of wool and cotton.

VYCRON: Brand name of polyester fiber, made by Beaunit Corporation.

VYRENE: A spandex fiber, made by U.S. Rubber Company. Technical description: a continuous monofilament polyurethane elastomer, with stretch and recovery characteristics.

WAFFLE CLOTH: Fabric with honeycomb weave; in cotton, identified as waffle piqué; sportswear, evening accessories.

WAISTCOAT: Vest, sleeveless and waist-length, worn under jacket for business, sports, formal wear. Can be single- or double-breasted, matching suit or of different fabric and color.

WALE: Yarns which run lengthwise in cloth weaving.

WARP PRINT: Woven fabric, plain filling and printed warp threads which achieve a shadow-effect design. Sometimes referred to as shadow print.

WASTE SILK: Unreeled filaments remaining before and after long filaments have been removed. Carded and often combed and spun.

WATER-REPELLENT: Quality of fabric produced by finishing process causing fabric to shed water but allowing air to circulate through fabric. Can be periodically renewed.

WATERPROOFING: Finishing process employed to close pores of fabric. Usually accomplished by use of rubber, oil or lacquer compounds.

WEAVE: Any process of forming fabric on loom by interlacing warp and filling threads with each other. Variations of basic principle are used for different types of fabrics.

WEFT: Yarn running crosswise in fabric. Synonym for filling yarn.

WEIGHTED SILK: Silk on which metallic salts are used in dyeing and finishing to increase weight and to give richer appearance.

WELLINGTON BOOT: High, waterproof boot.

WELT: Thin, strong strip of leather which joins upper and sole of a shoe.

WHIPCORD: Coarse, twill-weave fabric made of hard-twisted yarns. Solid colors. Used in sportswear and topcoats. Also called "elastique" for military uniforms.

WIDESPREAD COLLAR: Shirt collar with wide spread between points.

WIGAN: Stiff-finished, plain-weave cotton fabric used by tailors for interlinings and stiffening.

WINDSOR COLLAR: Widespread collar on shirt, attached or separate.

WINDSOR KNOT: Large-size double knot with special method of tying.

WING COLLAR: Standing collar on shirt with tabs or wings; worn with tailcoat or dinner jacket or for formal or seminormal day wear.

WING-TIP SHOE: Heavily perforated shoe with forward part designed as spread wing.

WOOF: Obsolete; see Weft

WOOL: Animal hair spun, woven, knitted or felted into fabric for clothing and accessories.

WOOL-DYED: Fabric manufactured of fiber dyed before spinning into yarn. Synonym for stock-dyed.

WORSTED: Smooth-surfaced fabric spun from long-staple, evenly combed wool; tightly woven, hard-finished.

YARN: Continuous strands of spun fiber, cleaned, drawn and twisted. Made of wool, silk, cotton, linen or manmade fibers. Used for weaving, knitting.

YARN-DYED: Fabric manufactured from yarns which are dyed before they are woven or knitted.

ZANTREL: Trademark of cellulosic staple rayon made by American Enka Corporation.

ZEFRAN: An acrylic fiber made by Dow Chemical Company.

ZEIN FIBERS: Fibers made into yarn or fabric, regenerated from protein base of cornmeal.

ZELAN: Trade name of water-repellent process by Du Pont.

ZEPEL: Fabric fluoridizer, a stain- and water-repellent finish, registered by Du Pont.

Z TWIST: Spirals in yarn or cord which conform to slope of middle part of letter Z. Referred to as right or regular twist.

INDEX

73 74 75 10 9 8 7 6 5 4 3 2 1